The

The Journey

An Egyptian Woman Student's Memoirs of America

by Radwa Ashour

Translated by Michelle Hartman

OLIVE
BRANCH
PRESS

An imprint of Interlink Publishing Group, Inc.
www.interlinkbooks.com

First published 2018 by

Olive Branch Press
An imprint of Interlink Publishing Group, Inc.
46 Crosby Street, Northampton, MA 01060
www.interlinkbooks.com

Originally published in Arabic by Dar Al-Adab, as *Al-Rihla: Ayyam Talibah Misriyah fi Amrika*, 1983.

Library of Congress Cataloging-in-Publication data available
ISBN-13: 978-1-62371-997-5

Printed and bound in the United States of America

To order our free 48-page, full-color catalog, please call us at
1-800-238-LINK, e-mail us at sales@interlinkbooks.com,
or visit our website www.interlinkbooks.com

The Journey

Chapter One

I left Cairo at dawn on August 30, 1973. I kissed my farewells and entered the customs area carrying a big blue suitcase filled with clothes, books, and a small handbag, which held my green Egyptian passport, my airline ticket, and a leather wallet. The wallet held some money and a few pictures of my family. One of these was a cartoon by Salah Jaheen. As children, we used to sing his song over and over again, a chorus accompanying the singer:

> *Soura, soura, soura*
> we all want our picture taken
> a picture of happy people
> under our victorious flag.

But now, like then, I have the same question: Can our generation freeze this moment in time, like a photograph taken under our victorious flag? That's why I've kept this beautifully laminated picture with me, along with one other, the one we took after the Six-Day War; it has burn marks on it because it reflects what we suffered after being charred by fire. Along with those two pictures, I kept a third, also of my family. It shows my father, at the front, imposing and stubborn—torn between his desire to let me go out into the world as an extension of himself and his role as a fearful Muslim man with country roots who wants girls to be sheltered. My mother is in the background, my siblings look enthusiastic, and there I am with a question on my face.

I wasn't carrying a picture of handsome, turban-wearing Shaykh Rifa'a with me, but I'm certain that he was somewhere in my consciousness even if I'd stopped paying close attention to him. I was, like him, on my way to seek knowledge in a country, "far-away from us, the furthest from consideration." But I was unlike him, too. I was leaving neither as a neutral person who doesn't know what she's faced with, nor like the generation of researchers who followed him—the ones who left and returned besotted with the bright lights of imperialism.

When the woman at the counter gave me back my passport and ticket, I waved my final farewells. I then went through to the departures area, sat down on a big black leather chair, and waited for my flight to be announced. My terrible toothache worsened during the long hours of waiting. It turned into a headache.

What year was this family picture of us taken? In 1962 or at the beginning of the following year? I remember that we'd sat in front of the photographer during the same week that I'd seen Djamila Bouhired speak at the University of Cairo. It was the first time I'd ever entered the university campus. The lights in the big lecture theater surprised me; the way they shone reminded me of a bride on her wedding night. We went on a school bus with two of our teachers. Djamila looked straight at us while talking. She was a small, thin woman wearing a simple, traditional dress, whose two-colored green and white background met in a seam with a red crescent atop it, an Algerian flag behind her.

We all applauded and this tiny woman spoke. Her speech affected me deeply, giving me guidance to find the right path in life.

I wondered if going abroad was the right decision. This damned toothache—I didn't know how I'd get rid of it. They announced that our flight was boarding. I sat down on the plane and fastened my seatbelt, preparing for takeoff. I looked out the window at the lavender enveloping the land and sky, recalling that it was at this very same lavender time of day, one year and seven months earlier, that the security forces imprisoned thousands of students who had staged a sit-in inside the lecture theaters at the university.

They had walked out in orderly rows singing the national anthem, "My Country, Biladi." And it was also at this same lavender time on another day when two young men and myself, on behalf of the Egyptian Writers and Artists Commission, walked up to the counter of the central post office on Adli Street to send telegrams to the president of the republic, the leader of the parliament, and the prime minister, protesting the imprisonment of the students. This lavender dawn was tender and sad. What compelled me to travel abroad? I stared out of the window and Farid appeared to me, looking handsome, smiling encouragingly with frightened eyes. My toothache intensified as the plane took off.

"University students should wait for the next stop," the driver announced as he pulled into town. The passengers all got off except me and the young man sitting next to the window in the row across from me. When the bus stopped again, it was the last stop, inside the university campus. I got off and the young man followed me. I also saw a young woman with thick eyebrows who must have been sitting somewhere behind me, because I hadn't seen her before. The driver gave us our suitcases and I looked around in order to figure out what to do next. The young man and woman had started having a conversation in a European language I didn't understand. I walked over to them and asked them in English if they were new students. When they responded that they were, I picked up my suitcase and walked beside them. We put our luggage in the Student Union storage area and then went to the administration building that had been described to us. We forgot to introduce ourselves, I thought, so I slowed my pace and said: "I'm from Egypt, my name is Radwa Ashour."

The young woman was Polish and the young man was Israeli. I was taken aback; I said nothing. We arrived at the foreign students' office and I sat down on a chair across from them, alone. When the young woman and man finished speaking with the person in charge of the office, I looked at him questioningly. Pointing at the two of them, he told me: "They're going to Prince House, the

3

graduate students' residence. I explained the way to them. We'll all meet there in the afternoon." He gave me an envelope with a map of the university, some pamphlets, as well as information about the town of Amherst, the University of Massachusetts, and the other universities in the area.

We went back to the Student Union to get our luggage, and then set off to look for Prince House. I started to worry about how heavy my suitcase was. I was about two or three paces behind Theresa, the Polish woman, who had started chatting with the young man. Eventually, we found the building but, not knowing how to get in, we started walking around it. Every time we thought that we'd discovered the entrance, it was just another locked door. It was the last day of August. The weather was hot, the humidity suffocating. I started dripping sweat and shifting my heavy suitcase from one hand to the other. Finally, we found the entrance.

The director of the house told me that I couldn't stay there because I hadn't sent a prior request and so I would have to sort myself out somewhere else, at least for a night or two. When the director of the International Students' Office arrived, he took me in his car to another student residence to find a room where I could stay for a night. The man was about thirty, polite, and friendly. He took a lot of care in how he dressed and looked like a turn-of-the-century British colonial functionary. His smooth blond hair was carefully parted to one side. He had rosy cheeks and shiny shoes. He wore a jacket and tie and spoke in a slow, crisp voice, careful to pronounce every word as if he were presenting an English language lesson on the radio. He looked odd, especially surrounded by students wearing shorts and blue jeans, most of them with messy long hair, hippie-style. To break the silence, I asked him: "Have you ever visited Egypt or any neighboring countries?"

"No, but I spent several years stationed in Indochina."

Never in my life had I believed in that old adage "silence is golden" as much as I did at that moment. But I felt like if I opened my mouth once more, he would have just casually added that he'd been a solider in Vietnam, carrying the banner of democracy into the jungles of Asia. Everything here had started off on the wrong note… In the morning, I'd met an Israeli and, in the evening, a dapper young man who spent "several years stationed in Indochina"! What was I doing here?

My first meeting was with the director of the Afro-American Studies Department with whom I'd only corresponded about my program of study a few times. Now that I had arrived, I would face a number of ironic and comical situations with him. I hadn't come here because I'd wanted to study in the United States particularly, but rather because of my very specific interest in Black American literature, about which I wanted to write my doctoral dissertation. In Egypt, I'd been advised to enroll in this particular degree program by Mrs. Shirley Graham Du Bois, the Black American writer and widow of the great leader whose last name she still carried. She was sure of its anti-colonial, liberation-oriented outlook and convinced by the structure of its teaching program. Mrs. Du Bois had given me the university's application form herself and written me a recommendation letter for a departmental scholarship, telling them that I was a serious Egyptian researcher, a professor at Ain Shams University, and a politically progressive writer. This friend of mine, who was over sixty, had told me that the department chair, Michael Thelwell, was a friend of hers. She thought that I would enjoy meeting him because of his intellectual qualities and exceptionally humane personality.

While sitting and waiting for my older friend's friend, I wondered if, like her, he was approaching his seventies. I didn't know if there was a retirement age for university professors in this country. "Here he is. He's come," said the department's administrator whose office I'd been waiting in.

A tall young man with a Ho Chi Minh beard walked over to me, extended his hand, and said, "Ms. Radwa Ashour." His hair was combed up in a neat Afro and he was wearing a loose, brightly colored African-print shirt. Around his neck hung a necklace with a small, ivory African mask on it. His skin was light brown, like mine. He had wide eyes with long eyelashes that closed over them when he was speaking as if he didn't want to see anything while he was talking, except what was in his head.

I didn't know if I felt alienated by this man's appearance because of my preconception that he would probably be a white-haired professor, carrying his years heavily, perhaps swaying corpulently and seeming shorter than he actually was. Or was it because of his unexpectedly untraditional appearance within this very traditional university context?

What compelled me to speak to him with a frankness that surprised even me? Was I overcome by feeling foreign simply because I was faced with someone who appeared different than I'd expected? Or did something about this man and the way he talked catch my attention and give me a feeling of familiarity? I told him that I had been wrestling with such a strong sense of alienation that I'd begun to feel afraid. I carried on by telling him that I wasn't sure about being here, I might just pack my bags and leave. I told him that I wanted to study Afro-American literature because of my interest in the relationship between literature and the reality of people's struggles. I also said that I taught in an English literature department, but didn't want to become someone so embroiled in their research that I spent my whole life studying things which are not at the heart of the urgent issues that matter to me—the most pressing causes of our times.

He listened to me and didn't speak much. He proposed some specific practical steps: I should meet the Director of Graduate Studies in the English Department, the department granting me my academic degree. I should then see if this very same professor might be the supervisor of my work. He continued: "I also suggest that you add a course in African literature to your schedule this semester. The Nigerian novelist Chinua Achebe is here and attending his lectures is an opportunity not to be missed."

As I left the department, my feelings of anxiety and alienation dissipated in the novelty of the situation, particularly because of the disparity between my mental image of the professor and the young man who I'd just met. I laughed as I wrote a letter to Mourid about it. At that time, I still didn't know that there was yet another ironic aspect to this situation—I had surprised this man as much as he had surprised me. Didn't the old woman say that I was a friend of hers? And didn't my official papers declare that I had finished a master's degree and had six years of teaching experience in the university?

Who was this, then, sitting across from him? In the fall of 1973, I was a petite young woman with a round face, symmetrical features, a very short, young boy's haircut and simple clothes, who looked barely twenty years of age!

Michael drove his red convertible with abandon, not paying attention to the speed even when zigzagging around the mountain roads with their sudden curves. We exchanged a few words at the beginning of the journey, then we fell silent. Despite a few small signs that we were on the threshold of autumn, we were over-whelmed by the total greenness of our surroundings. Yellow, orange, and red were all lost amid the thick green. This took me back to the house I was born in, overlooking the river. The Nile valley stretches up to the north because of the richness of the river and has become so green thanks to the toil of emaciated peasants who break their backs to cultivate the land. It stretches down to the south, only to be startled by the desert, which interferes with and overpowers it until it becomes only a narrow strip of green. I sat there, preoccupied. Was it isolation that I felt? Or the difficulty of connecting with this young Jamaican man absorbed in something far away that I didn't understand? We were on our way to a town near Amherst to meet the professor who Michael suggested could be the supervisor of my work.

This time the professor did not surprise me. He was a man in his sixties, with white hair and movements slowed down by the weight of the years carried on his body, although he was still active. He seemed to me to be a fully American professor with his checkered jacket, a silver bracelet, and rubber-soled shoes. We sat on a spacious balcony with nothing separating us from the wild plants of the forest except a wooden trellis that stretched along the balcony's walls to its roof. We spoke about my program of study without going into great detail. Before I left, this elderly American professor patted my shoulder, saying: "Try not to feel so isolated!" Did my face betray my timidity? The professor's words definitely surprised me and I was embarrassed that he'd noticed how much I didn't fit in—I hadn't realized that he could see it.

We got into the car to return to Amherst. On the road, Michael invited me to have dinner with him and I agreed. As he was stopping the car in front of a shop that sold fish, he asked me: "Do you like lobster?" "I don't know!" He got out and returned after a few minutes, carrying a big brown paper bag with some holes in it. I looked inside and I saw two big sea animals with long, moving legs ending in huge claws. Michael said, smiling: "Don't despair, I'll cook you something else!" We stopped in front of another shop in Amherst and bought meat, bread, and some vegetables. Then we went up the hill rising along the north side of the town, across the winding mountain roads among the towering trees whose thick, green, intertwined branches blocked out the sunlight. Finally, Michael stopped his car, announcing, "We've arrived!"

In the middle of the cloudy greenness and the impending dusk, the place looked beautiful and unusual to me. This silence that I was listening to resonated strangely, as if something completely new. Michael opened the door and I walked into a spacious kitchen, bathed in light. He washed his hands, filled two big pots with water and put them on the stove. He then seasoned the meat before putting it in the oven. I went next door into the living room, which had a sofa, several chairs, and a little table. Hanging on one wall was a giant black-and-white photograph of Che Guevara riding a horse in the jungle, his face glowing like the star on his black beret. On the next wall hung a neat, symmetrically arranged collection of small weapons—a rifle and two revolvers. Along the third wall were two wooden planks with books piled up on top of them, rising all the way up from the ground along its full length. I walked over to examine the titles of the books, leafing through some of them in order to push aside the question nagging at me.

The place was totally silent, confirming this secluded mountain house's complete isolation and triggering a strange feeling within me that kept asking: "What am I doing here?"

Was this simply a foreign young woman looking for a way to feel safe? Or was it a vague and deeply rooted anxiety derived from the old-fashioned idea that, when a man and a woman are alone, the third party is temptation? I went back into the kitchen and found Michael putting the lobsters into the first pot full of boiling water, just like that, whole and alive. He also put four ears of corn into the second pot to boil. He asked me: "What will you drink?" "Juice." "You won't drink something else?" "Just juice, thanks."

We sat down and ate in silence. Michael sat across from me, the picture of Che on his horse behind him. Why, right at that moment, did I think about Naguib Sorour as if he were a third person there with us? I saw him then just as he was before I had left Cairo, stern-faced and with a slight but obvious limp in one of his legs. Without planning it,

I started telling Michael about Abdel Nasser, the Six-Day War, my family disowning me for my marriage to someone they didn't approve of, the student protests, and the amazing love poem that Shaykh Imam sang about Alexandria, and in particular two specific lines which always gave me solace: "I feel like a student at the heart of this protest / who chanted your name, only to die celebrating." I'm sure I spoke about many topics that evening, or was it only one? I must have spoken quite a lot, how else could I have been able to talk about the suffering of a generation that was thrust from these energetic chants into the hell of the Six-Day War, its massacres, and their ashes?

When we got in the car so Michael could drive me back to Prince House, I felt relaxed because I'd lightened the load I was carrying. I turned to him suddenly and said, smiling: "It's true. Perhaps we will be burned by the flames and become ashes. But perhaps the fire will make us more mature and we will rise from it like prophets or loaves of bread in the oven!"

When we got back to Prince House, I said, "Wait here one minute!" I went up to my room and returned with a small wooden box inlaid with mother-of-pearl that I had bought in Cairo. I handed it to Michael through the car window, saying with a smile: "I imagined you much older than me and when I found out that we were close in age, I was too embarrassed to give you the gift that I'd brought to you from Egypt. Now everything is different— We've become friends, no?"

To the outside observer, I was a model of quick and easy adaptability to my new reality. I was good at English, I found connecting with people easy, and I like both to chat and to listen to other people chat. Within a week of my arrival, I knew a lot of students, both Americans and foreigners. But despite this, my inner anxieties got the better of me, since everything seemed strange and different. From the moment I walked through the glass doors at Logan Airport in Boston, I knew I'd stepped out into a new world.

Even the way the rain fell was new to me—it rained heavily on a scorchingly hot day at the end of August. I was sitting in a taxi, watching the relentless back and forth of the car's windshield wipers against the rain, and dripping with sweat from the heat and humidity.

When I first got to the university, classes hadn't begun yet. Most of the male students were wearing just shorts. The female students added tiny cotton blouses hardly as big as your hand, leaving their bellies and backs exposed to the sun. They sometimes walked around barefoot, exchanging passionate kisses in public. Although this amusing scene didn't offend me or my beliefs, I was certain that I was far away, so very far away, from everything known and familiar. And I was alone.

I was in my room in Prince House, days after my arrival, when someone knocked at my door and a middle-aged woman entered, carrying suitcases. She nodded at me, walked in, put down what she was carrying, and left. Then a man came in carrying things, too. The woman returned a second time with more things in her arms. They carried on like this, coming and going, until I realized that the woman must be my roommate.

But it wasn't so. At last, a tall, thin blonde woman appeared. We introduced ourselves. Then she busied herself with the two people who clearly were her parents, arranging her things: putting her clothes in drawers, her sheets and covers on the bed, and a typewriter and reams of unopened paper on the desk. I gathered that, despite how young Louisa was, she must have been at the stage of typing up her doctoral dissertation. I didn't deduce this solely from the extraordinary amount of paper that she put next to the typewriter on the desk, but rather from the obvious self-sacrifice and affection in her parents' behavior. The man and woman said goodbye to me and left.

Louisa went out with them. When she returned she was carrying a cotton teddy bear, a child's toy the size of a well-built toddler, and put it on her bed. As soon as she sat down, I asked her: "What's your area of specialization, Louisa?" "Physical education." "Sorry?"

But I had heard right. Louisa had come to university to study physical education. She was southern, from Maryland she later told me. This was her first time coming to Amherst and she informed me that her father's ancestors had Portuguese royal blood. "And my mother's ancestors…"

I didn't hear the rest of what she was saying; I finally had understood why she looked down on me and acted so conceited. She never spoke to me unless I asked direct questions, and she would always respond extremely politely, reinforcing the distance between us. The next morning, she woke up very early to the sound of the alarm clock and ate by herself silently. In the evening, she put her cotton teddy bear under her head, laid down in bed, and read the Bible. Only once did Louisa initiate a conversation with me. She seemed anxious, nervous, and apprehensive as she asked me: "What is your religion?" "I come from a Muslim family." Total silence. Louisa's presence in the room only made me feel more lonely. I sometimes asked myself: "Have I lost my mind to have traded my house in Cairo and Mourid's companionship for this white American southerner and her cotton teddy bear?"

I waited for a letter from Cairo. I kept waiting every day, despite all my calculations which told me that it couldn't possibly have arrived yet. Hadn't I sent my address only after I'd arrived? Didn't the address have to arrive there first before a response could come? Wouldn't the letter take at least a week to reach Cairo and another for a letter to return from there? I kept in mind how illogical my stubbornness was. I simply had to wait. But I had a persistent need to do something daily in the shadow of this letter. Even if it never came, anticipation loomed at just the prospect of it. This was the beginning of my relationship with the little mailbox with my room number—224—on it on the ground floor of Prince House. Each day I checked it several times, looking through its tiny glass window, not seeing anything, and then opening it just to be sure. I found it empty and then I left. Was I afraid? At that time I wasn't yet aware of the extent of my fear, but I did know that I was anxious. It seemed to me that Mourid and I, who had already lived in the shadow of a disjointed geography for so long, might be lost in our separation this time. A boy and a girl… yes, lovers. But each of us had taken somewhat different paths in this big, wide, and constantly unstable world. Seven years had passed since we'd become friends, and we'd been married for three. In Cairo, after we'd discussed my winning a scholarship to study abroad, and I'd accepted it, I felt that perhaps my friends and family were right and it was really stupid to leave the warmth of home: "A home is made by the connections between places and friends and the man you love. And yet off she goes, just like that!"

The six envelopes piled on top of each other on our brown desk contained our old letters, our stories from throughout the three years before we were married, when we would see each other only for one month each year. How many envelopes would we add to this, how many letters? The very idea made me ill, and I was so upset that I needed to lie down in bed and call for a doctor.

But actually, I was not sick but afraid, even terrified. I felt like a warrior who betrays himself by surrendering the minute he sees the face of his adversary. I told myself that I was going to back out of the offer to study in America, but I didn't. I went.

A week after my arrival, the university administration announced that new students should come to the Student Center the following day to have their photos taken for their university ID cards. I went to the building at the time I was supposed to. A light rain was falling through the humidity. At the Center, I waited in a long line in a narrow corridor, feeling suffocated by the mix of heat and humidity. Eventually it was my turn. The photographer took my picture and I left.

A few days later I got my university ID. It had a small color picture, just a tiny bit bigger than a postage stamp, showing a young woman with short, unkempt hair and big, glaring eyes. If you looked at this picture, you might think she was a stupid or completely terrified young woman. A look of confused anxiety destroys any of her face's possible beauty.

Chapter Two

When I woke up one autumn morning in October, I planned to go down to the shopping mall to buy a typewriter. The sky was clear and the weather was not yet very cold, so I decided to go on foot. I left the house but didn't turn onto the street that would lead me into the valley. Instead I walked toward a street I liked that continued on from the university into the town of Amherst. It was a street that didn't have any walls around it. When I arrived at the university in the summer, the branches of the trees planted all along the sides of the road were intertwined in a calm green composition impenetrable by sunlight. But now the branches had started losing some of their leaves and sunlight had started infiltrating through them, reaching the ground with shadows creeping toward each other to create bright and dark spaces.

I recalled the poet Abu Tayyib al-Mutanabbi's phrase "dinars slipping through fingertips," but the crunch of dry leaves under my footsteps led my mind away from him to look instead at the piles of leaves surrounding me, and scattered around the tree trunks, as if they belonged there—leaves of yellow, gold, brown, and the color of mulch. I turned and took the road that led downhill toward town. Because of the steepness of the slope, my body rushed forward and I felt a powerful blaze shoot through me. I started running in response to the incredible beauty of the place. The trees just amazed me. I slowed to a walk, only to respond to the autumn glow by running once again. I'd never seen trees like this in all my life. It wasn't simply the sheer number of trees, the many different types of trees, or even the number of leaves that lent this place such a glow. It was rather the diversity and number of colors on the branches of a single tree. Shy green leaves, like at the beginning of spring; bright green, harsh yellow and soft yellow, riotous orange, henna red and rust red, light brown and dark brown and murky, deathlike brown leaves. All of existence was there in one single tree, a celebration of color. What could be more freeing than all this brilliance? You can't think about it too much… So I stopped. Then I started again and ran like a colt, a child, a woman who truly loves the glory of life when it is excessively beautiful.

I walked for nearly an hour before I reached the central square near the shops. The sun shone on the roofs of the cars parked there. I looked behind me and saw the university buildings atop the hill, like different-sized matchboxes, strewn here and there, obviously incompatible with the place.

After I finished my shopping, I looked at the road rising up in front of me and thought, "So here I am. And I haven't thought about how to get back home. I'll break my back before getting there, but I guess I have to try." I walked a few minutes but I was exhausted. The typewriter I'd just bought wasn't light, even though it was the small kind you can carry in its own case. I stopped on the side of the road, stretched out my arm, and put my thumb up in the air—despite all the warnings I'd heard that hitchhiking could be dangerous and there'd been many violent incidents. What could happen to me on such a clear day, just a couple of miles from the university campus? A car stopped. "Are you headed to UMass?" One of the passengers responded in the affirmative. I opened the car door, saying, "I'll get out at the top of the hill." When I got out of the car after less than five minutes, I had another reason to be happy about having saved the effort of walking up the mountain—the astonished looks of the three American men in the car. Probably my confident, even commanding, tone wasn't what they were expecting from a foreigner, all the more so since I wasn't a European, or even a man!

As soon as I had gotten over certain discomforts, my inner child conquered my shyness, reminding me of my active, but long-gone, glory days when excitement and enthusiasm drove everything I did. That's what happened to me on that autumn day. The trees weren't the only reason. I'd started to get used to the place and form some connections to it.

My roommate Louisa moved out two weeks after I arrived. I felt much more relaxed being alone in the room without this descendant of Portuguese royalty, whom I discovered shrank from me for other reasons too. This white Southern girl was afraid of me, nervous about the color of my skin, my religious background, my nationality. In short, she was simply afraid of who I was and that I existed in the world. Was this Louisa afraid that I would get up in the middle of the night, beat a tam-tam, and then devour her alive? Was she afraid that I would wring her neck while she was sleeping? Or was this foolish girl afraid that I would seize the opportunity to use her typewriter when she went out? I don't know which of these scared Louisa the most, but the important thing was that she withdrew from the university and I felt calmer.

Letters from Egypt began to arrive. Two letters from Mourid came at the same time. My little mailbox had been good to me and I didn't forget this, even when I opened it and found nothing inside. Two letters at the same time, two days later another letter, and then a letter from a girlfriend of mine. I would shut the mailbox door gently and open a letter, reading it while bounding up the stairs towards my room on the second floor. Sometimes I would even stand in front of the mailbox and read a letter for the first time before going to a lecture.

Mourid's words were a kiss on my forehead blessing me. I had left worried. Hovering on the threshold, I'd asked myself if my journey wasn't merely an extra burden that Mourid didn't need. He couldn't return to Palestine—and having a home isn't the same thing as having a homeland, even if it's where you live. He was enthusiastic about me traveling and encouraged me to do it. But I also knew that when he went home each night, turned the key in the lock, opened the door and entered, that he would be overcome by loneliness. How could I fix this? In his letter he had written, "My homeland left a second time, when you left." He didn't know that his letters became a homeland for me when I was away from home. They made me feel that I was no longer lost in outer space, a place whose rules and customs I didn't know. The envelopes with letters inside began to pile up and this was not so sad. Weren't we continuing our conversations and beginning a new chapter?

The steps that I had been taking backward became one shy step forward, then two. The little woman started responding and learning.

I started reading history and literature voraciously, entering emotionally challenging fields of knowledge: reliving the suffering of the African continent whose open wounds have bled for hundreds of years. Forty million Africans stuffed onto ships where they were the merchandise, the cargo. They were branded at slave castles, piled up in overcrowded ships destined for the new world. Their lives there started on the auction block. Buying and selling, goods and merchandise. The machine moves, swallows and produces. Many slaves tilled the land. A master in a white plantation house with pillars. Huge fields of cotton, tobacco, and sugar cane. A machine that swallows up life and keeps going. The slaves sang, "Sometimes I feel / like a motherless child / a long ways from home." A slave runs away in the middle of the night. A slave conspires secretly. Slaves at times take a terrible oath: We will even kill our own newborn babies because they will grow up one day and the racist law will make them property. But they are killed. Blood and violence win in this new world; exile continues on. The slaves talk about one young enslaved man who battled the devil in his life, died, and went to heaven, but wasn't let in. So then he went to hell, and he wasn't let in, so he took his torch and wandered through the universe across time. Generations pass by and exile continues, trains carry Black families to the north, fleeing boll weevils and control by their masters. Slavery is now in the past. These people are free according to the laws and civil codes.

But the machine continues to swallow and produce. A Black man is beaten to death. Another whispers at dawn. Groups of Black people and fire sweeping all through the place, like trees burning during a storm. Exile continues as does this blood-red fire.

I read African literature and the history of the continent's civilizations. It expands and multiplies before me. Its only borders are the blue sea. Time passes by with its burdens, like the three rivers: the Nile, Niger, and Congo. I ford right into time and belong to this place. A small pair of scissors cuts a piece of black paper into the shape of Africa. I stick this black shape onto a green background. I draw the map of the continent on a white piece of paper with a pencil and outline its geography—the borders of its countries. Then I stick this on a red background. I ravenously read about so many things that I previously knew nothing about.

Spaces opened up and became more defined for me; I could see the masses moving by swiftly and dams blocking the path to the river. This dam is crumbling. This dam will be breached. I witness these fast-moving masses, my heart fears bloodshed, and then it sings hallelujah! I learn... from its swift movement over dewy grass that follows an apprehensive, contracted silence stuck to a tree trunk. I was startled by a squirrel, an animal new to me. I learned that like a mouse, it is ugly in silent stillness but its swift movements have an amazing, beautiful flow.

One night I went to a Duke Ellington concert; it was the first time I'd heard live jazz. I tried unsuccessfully to make the link between the older man in his seventies sitting down at the piano and the tunes emanating from the movement of his hand and the other instruments he was conducting. Did he make the music or did it make him? What rhythm filled the room and made the old man's body move as he played? Were these the beats of the seventy years he'd lived or of the music? Or was this rhythm the sound of captivity? The saxophone had a visibly and audibly wounded soul.

Finally, I started to reclaim some feeling of contentment and the ability to be boisterous. That's why, when I found myself in the middle of those incandescent trees on that warm autumn day, I was glowing with energy and took off running like a colt or a little girl.

I arrived back at Prince House carrying my typewriter, turned into the area where the mailboxes were, and heard the residence director, Mrs. Robinson, calling out to me, from in front of her room at the end of the hallway. When I reached her, she was back in her usual spot behind her desk and she said to me, "Robert and his wife called you and expressed how sorry they were about the outbreak of the war between Egypt and Israel. I too am sorry about that news; I hope you aren't too worried."

For a moment it all seemed like an absurd nightmare: this woman with her high-pitched voice, her skinny, brittle body, her office, and her room. What war? Sorry for what? Who is Robert? I ran to find the only other Arab student in the residence. "What's happening?" We dialed the radio through all of the stations.

When the 1967 war broke out, I was in a classroom at Cairo University, taking a Latin exam. In the background I could hear spirited songs, Gamal Abdel Nasser's speeches, and a generally patriotic atmosphere. The media was presenting this as a clash with Israel that would mean us reclaiming our rights and defeating the invaders. It was as if the armies slowly advancing towards occupied Palestine meant their victory in liberating it, and as if this war meant celebration or at least the promise of celebrations. Therefore, I wasn't too worried when I heard the sound of shelling while writing the answers on my exam paper. When I left the examination room and learned about the clashes between the armies, I was filled with enthusiasm. So what was happening now that made me feel overwhelmed with fear and worry? Had I unconsciously started to mix war and loss? Was it the isolation of being a foreigner in a faraway land? Or was it a rational feeling that our leaders would not be able to guide the country onto safe ground? I was seized by fear and from that day on I stayed in my room, too shy to face other people.

I waited for a telephone call from Egypt that never came. The American media besieged us. In a television special, Golda Meir did a walkabout through an area with three- and four-story buildings. Could that be Suez? The television announcer said it was Suez! The *New York Times* had a front-page photo of Egyptian soldiers imprisoned by an Israeli soldier guarding them from atop a raised platform. The bottom of the picture showed the Israeli's shoe and the butt of his rifle at the level of the Egyptians' heads. We didn't know for sure about being able to cross and destroy the Bar-Lev line, but the news of a gap in it reached us.

There were only ten Arab students in this American university of more than 20,000 students. Of the ten, we were reduced by three—one was always dishonest, the other two were women controlled by a man who was the husband of one and the brother of the other. (The two of them went to and from their lab together at the university and God help them if they deviated from this routine at all.) Because of our small numbers, we decided to form a committee that would be open to others and include any university students who wanted to participate. When we formed the committee, we had students who were new leftists, communists and Trotskyites, Afro-Americans, Puerto Ricans and also students from Africa and Latin America. This is how we formed the Committee to Defend the Rights of the Arab and Palestinian People, as part of Third-World student activism on university campuses at the time.

The committee met for the first time in a small room in the student union. Most of us sat on the floor, some others stood, and the rest sat on the few chairs we had. There was a young man sitting on the floor who belonged to the youth organization of the communist party. He wore a dark blue jean jacket with a round medal badge pinned to it, with a picture of the raised fists of black, white, and red arms. He had a bushy beard, rumpled hair tucked behind his ears with a thin black string, and a red scarf tied around his neck like a time-weathered sailor. His delicate features and worried eyes revealed his thin and even frail build. He was very young—not more than twenty—and extremely sweet in his interactions with others.

Sitting across from him on the floor were three young Trotskyite men, a young woman, and two other young men who you could tell were hippies. They wore old, dark-colored clothes. The young woman wasn't wearing a bra and the men's tangled hair hung to their shoulders. They were talking about their rejection of Israel as a settler-colonial state.

A tall, thin American man from one of the Black groups on campus stood against the wall; his beautiful facial features and brilliant Africanness showed through in his care for the clothes he was wearing. He was confident in his beauty and strength.

There were Ethiopian men standing with him against the wall, their faces an amazing summary of the ancient relationship between the African continent and the Arab peninsula. They had not taken special care with their clothes, but pride and self-esteem shone in their eyes. They spoke calmly and with organizing experience.

Pedro was the only Latin American student at this first meeting. He was a friendly, bubbly young man who it turned out was of Palestinian origin.

"My grandfather is from Palestine."

"What's your grandfather's name, Pedro?"

His face blushed and he quickly responded, "Not my actual grandfather, but his father."

We Arab students were spread throughout the room and participated in conversations in order to focus upon a number of agreed-upon points to include in a founding manifesto to be published in the university's daily newspaper, the *Daily Collegian*. We were seven Arab students: three Egyptians, two Sudanese, a Palestinian and a Lebanese. It was clear that some Arab students were not that tolerant of how the committee was formed. One person even said in a somewhat angry tone before leaving the room,

"We must decide if this is an Arab committee or one for any Black person or random communist." It was obvious that our colleague had suddenly become afraid of finding himself among people he distrusted on a racist, classist basis or for political reasons. Because of this, he found himself between a rock and a hard place—he wanted their work and support and at the same time wished they weren't there! Perhaps the others felt as he did too, but they didn't express themselves in the same way.

We made our position clear in our manifesto and in a number of letters to the editor. We focused on our opposition to Israel. We were not anti-Semitic, opposed to, or hostile towards Jews; ours was a rejection of Zionism and a settler-colonial state whose interests were linked to Imperial interests. We began alternating shifts at an information table in the campus center. Our plan was not only to disseminate publications and sell books, but also more fundamentally to answer questions about our cause and discuss things with anyone who wanted to engage in a conversation.

The general atmosphere in the room was diverse and energetic. The center gave a table and space to anyone who asked. Near us was a young woman with a display of leather belts for sale, which she had made and engraved designs on with a knife. There was another table of students who poured colored wax into molds of different shapes and sold them as candles. Other tables had political publications of one kind or another. For example, another table had publications by advocates for the rights of homosexuals and behind this was still another where a young hippie man was selling the small copper pipes used to smoke marijuana.

The building in the center of the campus had been recently designed to accommodate student activities and other services. It was a giant ten-story building, two floors of which were underground. It housed the student union offices, meeting rooms, halls for concerts and movie screenings, shops displaying everything from books to toothpaste, a barbershop, a print shop, a post office, a pinball arcade, stalls selling cigarettes and candy, and two coffee shops that sold fast food and drinks. The upper floors of the building housed a restaurant, a bar, and a hotel for university guests. Activity in the student center didn't quiet down until the middle of the night.

We set up our table with publications near one of the entrances. Some people stopped to ask questions or discuss things with us. Quite often, a young man or woman would come up to us and start talking with some version of "I am a Jewish man," or "I am a Jewish woman," out of curiosity, apprehensiveness, or provocation. They would say, "Yes, but…"

I would wait for what was coming next. At the beginning, many of them seemed to think our measured responses were evidence of our maliciousness, a political ploy, or us simply being diplomatic. But they gradually began to believe what we were saying about the fact that we weren't opposed to Jews as Jews, and that we were firm in distinguishing between Judaism as a religion and Zionism as a political dogma.

This was the case for most Jewish students. The Zionists, on the other hand, were full of hatred towards us. The most antagonistic of these was a young man from the Jewish Defense League. They were a group who walked around campus wearing skullcaps and rectangular cloth armbands emblazoned with the blue and white Israeli flag. Whenever they saw one of us, they would stop and stare in blatant, hostile provocation. None of them ever dared to hit us, fearing for their academic future. Nonetheless, they had ways to let us know that they were there and prepared to eradicate us at any moment. For example, one of them stood across from the speaker at one of our meetings for almost two hours, staring at him, with his body swaying right and left. They used to stand for hours in front of our table, not saying a word but simply staring at us to terrorize us. Their hatred for us increased with their ignorance, and we would simply carry on with our work. One member of our group would replace another, taking turns until four in the afternoon, when we gathered up all of our publications, put them into a large cardboard box, gave our table back, and left for the day.

I had learned to conquer my earliest childhood fears and was able to use every experience I had to emerge with my head held high. I grew up with three brothers whom I always feared would be associated with bravery and courage because they were boys, while I would be associated with weakness and fear because I was not. So I used to plunge headlong into things. I would always be the one to reach out and take the first shot and then claim it didn't hurt... I never squirmed when swallowing bitter medicine; I would swallow it with feigned calm, claiming that it wasn't so bitter. I would bet my eldest brother that I could carry as much as he could... I didn't show my fear when I had to go into a dark room. I don't know exactly what traces this childhood stubbornness and assertiveness left on my later behavior, but I know that I gained a measure of moral courage and bravery from it.

In this American university where I was living and studying, however, I experienced an insistent fear for the first time since my very early childhood. Those Zionists succeeded in arousing a deep anxiety inside me. Would one of them attack me with a large bat and bash my head in? The violence in the look of that young guy from the Jewish Defense League made me wonder what kind of harm his hatred might translate to. America did not make me feel safe at all. The posters hanging everywhere on campus only increased these feelings of insecurity—for example, one for young women that announced, "If you are assaulted, call one of the following telephone numbers." According to the statistics they gave us, a rape happens in the United States every eleven minutes. The director of Prince House, Mrs. Robinson, was afraid to go out after dark. Should I be afraid as well? This woman was paralyzed by fear. Deciding to stay in at certain hours would not make me feel less afraid, I decided. But at night, when the campus was almost deserted and I felt a group of young men walking behind me, I would slow down and let them pass before I would relax. Then I could see them and observe how they were behaving. On drizzly days, or when it was raining, I felt safer. My umbrella had a big stick attached to it, suitable for defending myself if need be.

Chapter Three

I am in a permanent state of motion. As a child I had an overflow-ing, consistently powerful life force and was always on the move. As an adolescent, I kept moving for fear of my developing body and my impending confinement to the home as a woman. As an adult I moved so much so that I could remain equal to men my age. I kept moving so I could learn, I kept moving so I could be free, I kept moving so my family wouldn't envelop me in their love and regulations. I stayed in motion so that society wouldn't force me into the inferior compartments it confines women to, and eventually all this movement became second nature. This was how it had been since I arrived in America. I found myself still constantly moving in order to ward off the feeling of being a stranger and to fulfill the many academic requirements that would allow me to finish my degree quickly so I could go back to Egypt. I attended my assigned courses. I read, wrote, discussed, explained, and passed my time well—always on the move.

Something unanticipated sometimes occurred, however. Then everything went still. Once I was running across the street holding two books that I'd just bought when suddenly it felt like I was fall-ing from a high wall, rolling down it with a half-formed question hanging on my lips: "Why?"

There was some kind of fuss happening. I looked around. I was in the street, lying on the ground. People I didn't know were stand-ing around me, staring. There was one face I did know. I fixed on it and called out, "Hi, Pedro!" Slowly I became aware that there had been some kind of accident. The distinctive siren of an ambulance wailed. People carried me to it. Someone I didn't know sat next to me, asked me my name, and I answered.

"Your address?"

"Room 224, Prince House."

"Your family's address?"

"My family doesn't live in this country."

The man insisted, and I grew tired, telling myself that he was stupid; he couldn't possibly imagine how to contact Cairo and tell them I'd been hit by a car. I didn't respond. My body hurt as the ambulance lurched down the street. Why did they carry me out this way, flat on my back on a stretcher? I closed my eyes.

And then there I was again, lying flat on my back. When? A bright light. They were examining me. Was this the university hospital? I heard someone saying "concussion" but I didn't know what that meant. Was I unconscious, asleep, or did they give me anesthesia? I didn't know. I didn't remember. It was morning when I'd gone out to buy books. Now it was nighttime. There was a little lamp next to me, but the room was dark. A young man and woman dressed in white were there. When I noticed their presence, I looked right at them and they both smiled at me. Then I no longer felt their presence. Was I asleep? Here they were again. The young woman put a thermometer in my mouth and the young man took my blood pressure. I slept and woke with them there again, taking my temperature and blood pressure. They came and went. Were they waking me up, or was I waking up at the sound of their footsteps? Did they always come in together? Or was it once just the young man and the next time just the young woman, but it simply seemed to me that they always walked in together? Was I asleep or unconscious?

The next morning I was feeling better. The nurses here were devoted and friendly; they moved me to another bed near a window where I could see part of the hill. So this was the university hospital, and I could see treetops through the window of my room.

It was the beginning of November; the winter hadn't truly arrived yet and the trees hadn't completely lost their leaves. I looked out at them while resting on my right side.

One of my housemates from Prince House came to visit me in the afternoon, and she brought some of my clothes with her. After that, my Arab colleagues came. One of them joked while saying hello, "Of course, you aren't used to walking among cars, and camels don't hit pedestrians!" Then another finished his thought, also laughing, "What are your impressions of urban life far from the desert?" The first one came back sarcastically with, "You should first ask her about crocodiles and if they attack people bathing in the river."

I replied, "Well, I have an incident that beats all of these jokes. When we arrived, the office for foreign students put on a concert for us and there was a new student from Germany. An American woman, I don't know what planet she came from, went over to her and asked her with profound interest, 'Do you have telephones in Germany?' The young German woman's shock at the question prevented her from being able to answer and the American woman felt badly because she thought she'd embarrassed the German woman with her question, understanding that there were no telephones in Germany. And so she was quiet and didn't say anything else."

My guests laughed at the story and one of them said, still giggling, "Come on, you're lying. It's true they're ignorant and shut off from the world, but not to that extent. Admit that you made that story up!"

Smiling, I told him, "That's what I heard. Don't ask me; blame the person who told me."

I felt much better than the day before, and I no longer could complain of any specific pains. I was stuck on bed rest and filled with increasing gratitude for everything around me. I'd been hit by a car, banged my head, and the accident could have been life threatening. But now I was fine and filled with feelings of gratitude. When the nurse told me that they'd run tests on me the following day before discharging me from the hospital, I was calm and content.

When I left the hospital the sun was shining, adding a certain sparkle to the place, along with the special warmth of a bright autumn day. My friend who had come to be with me when I was discharged said, "They're all waiting for you in the car!" We turned the corner and found an Iranian friend of ours waiting next to his car with half a dozen of our other friends. They all greeted me, shook my hand, and kissed me. We went back to Prince House, the car transforming into one of those shared taxis which moved people between different regions in Egypt, carrying double the number of passengers it should, all of us talking boisterously. Laughing, I said, "The only thing this car is missing is the baskets!"

This is how we arrived at Prince House, entering in a victory procession. "Didn't we make it back here safely?" one of my friends commented seriously.

I had begun to feel I belonged at Prince House by getting to know the people there—from the director, who stood at the door of her room on the ground floor, poking her little head out of her hole with curious anxiety from time to time, like a mouse, to the people responsible for cleaning the floor I lived on. There were two of them who were like sitcom characters. One was short and fat and laughed silently as if swallowing his laughter. The other was tall and talked in a low-pitched voice, suddenly exploding in loud laughter, which would make his huge lower jaw jiggle. I'd also made friends with some students whom I slowly began to trust and rely on, as well as many acquaintances with whom I had warm and friendly encounters. All of us shared the experience of waiting for the mail to be delivered. Each of us would stand in front of our own little mailbox and wait for the short, round, dark-skinned woman who was responsible for delivering the letters, who would appear every day like a moving apparition behind the glass doors of the mailboxes. She would slide the letters the postman had just delivered into our little boxes.

I got a new roommate who did not have royal blood running through her veins; this was the first thing I was thankful for. Anita was twenty-eight years old, one year older than me, and she was studying for a PhD in nutrition. As soon as she learned I was Egyptian, she told me how very happy that made her because her mother's father was of Syrian origin. She then put this aside and sat down to tell me about her family tree, as Americans so often do. She said that her grandfather had emigrated from Syria when he was young and worked as a merchant. He made good money and got married to an Italian Catholic woman, who became her grandmother. Then came the Great Depression in 1929, during her mother's childhood, which led to her grandfather's bankruptcy. He died in anguish.

"My grandfather's name was Tawfiq."—she pronounced it Tufik—"Isn't that an Arabic name?"

After having enthusiastically uncovered our shared origins, she then moved on to a new topic in her monologue. "My father is a Mormon. The Mormons are a group…" The young woman was good-hearted and quick to empathize, like people from the countryside. She was conservative in her behavior and ways of interacting with people, especially compared to other American girls her age. She brought things normally hidden out into the open and despite her relatively young age to have made such academic progress, she wasn't at all afraid or worried about anyone pointing out that she hadn't gotten married yet.

After having lived for nearly three months in this student residence, I found I had regained my ability to enjoy my role as a spectator. When the scene I was watching was very strange and new to me, I would at first be frightened. Then I would move to passive, astonished, and anxious apprehension—the fascination of a person watching a film for the first time—that marks the distance between the spectator and what they are watching.

On my way from the library to Prince House, I would always reassure myself by looking for a message in my mailbox. I would turn the dial of the padlock to number 7, then to the left side until the letter L, and then the door to this little treasure chamber would open, with a letter for me, or sometimes even more than one! If I didn't find anything, I'd leave quickly.

One day I spotted a pile of papers through the little glass window. Were they official papers from the university administration? Or advertisements? As I turned the lock to open the box, I was so worried that I could hear my heart beating loudly. They were letters… Airmail letters! I took out five rectangular envelopes with my name and address written on them in Mourid's neat, clear handwriting. I walked slowly towards the stairs leading back to my room. The sealed envelopes I was holding were a gift that overwhelmed me, like the flowers my son Tamim would give me years later, when he had not yet reached two, with the words, "I love you, Mama, and because I love you I brought you a rose!" A woman receives five letters written to her by the man she loves and they all arrive together when she is far away from home. Which should I open first? I opened them all together. Then, a great treat—they were poems. I was taken by surprise, as if I didn't know that Mourid was a poet or as if I hadn't already received dozens of new poems from him by post. In any case, I began to read:

Just as water enters the depth of stones
In our village in wintertime
A thousand paths inside the mountaintops cleave to this water
And dwell in it like a fox standing watch
Listening to the farmers' footsteps and
The ploughs tilling the land year after year
He emerges a river, a spring, and a fountain pouring forth water
And announces like a child
Here I am! I have arrived, come and drink
The dove drinks from it, so do the people of the village
Caravans stop there and a bunny rabbit plays

The land is rich with oranges
Roses grow red there, new fruits ripen
This is how your love enters me
And illuminates the lines of this poem!

Two days later, three more envelopes arrived with the remaining parts of the poem. It was now five hundred lines long. If the poem had been written by someone else for another woman, I would have held onto it and shot out of my room like an arrow to show it to my friends. But the poem was written for me. It was a magic mirror that Mourid had made for me himself, from a long distance. He'd announced, "This is for you!" Is this really me? The Radwa in the poem was pure, clear, blue fire. I stood in front of her, torn between modesty and pride. I still do.

I carried the poem in my heart, in my classrooms in the English and Afro-American Studies departments, in the library, in the student center, and at home.

In the English department, I moved around inside whiteness: white faces dominated and even the long corridors were painted in light colors. In the evening, when we would leave the classroom heading for the exit, its corridors were cold, lonely, and depressing despite being heated. Their weak light gave off the pallor of somebody dying.

In contrast, the building in which the Afro-American Studies department was housed was warmer than usual. By the time I'd reach the classrooms on the third floor I would be dripping with sweat. The walls were painted bright colors—green, blue, and orange, even the black shone. In addition to the department, this building also had a daycare for children of students and workers, a special center for Third-World students, and artists' workshops. In this university building it was normal to see little Black and Latino children going up and down the stairs, and it wasn't unusual to hear the sound of a saxophone or drums wafting up from the ground floor where the ateliers were. I got used to this place, even to Sango, the giant wolfhound that one of the professors brought to class and tied to the window with a leash during lectures. I walked through the classrooms and corridors of the building with ease, feeling that I knew it and was connected to it.

The way other people receive you always makes an impact on you, and it takes on even greater significance when you are far from home. In this department, unlike some distant, remote university, everyone liked me—they welcomed me because I had come to them from Egypt. Surely we were able to form this immediate, close connection because of how deeply they felt they were Africans who had been deracinated for centuries and still somehow belonged to Egypt. Thus, I was not a stranger, but another Egyptian among them.

They had pride in the accomplishments of both ancient and modern Egypt. They found the brilliance of ancient Egyptian civilization to be related to the continent they belonged to by heritage and origin. Abdel Nasser's Egypt and the national liberation movement extended and renewed that support. The Harlem Renaissance of the 1920s amplified the voices of freedom fighters who called for the rights of Black people and their liberation. It was based upon the civilizations of the African continent: Egyptian, Ethiopian, and the kingdoms of West Africa. This was a response to white America's aspersions claiming that the Africans they brought to the new world by force were primitives, with no history, living on a dark continent that had never known civilization.

The department, like others that had a clear national liberation orientation, chose to call itself the W. E. B. Du Bois Department of Afro-American Studies. This name was in homage to Du Bois, the father of African unity starting in 1904, who fought for it in both writing and action. He was persecuted in the McCarthy era and was stripped of his American passport until Nkrumah made a formal, official request of the United States government after Ghanaian independence. When I was in the States, Du Bois had been an iconic figure for nearly ninety years and had a full history behind him as a researcher, creator, and foundational figure.

The storm of American terrorism against him never brought him down; he kept calling for the liberation of his people—Black people—in America and for the liberation of Africa and its people from colonization and exploitation. He died and was buried in the soil of Ghana.

Chapter Four

"It's snow!"

Little white flakes kept drifting down from the sky until the ground looked like the kind of holiday cakes my mother sprinkled with powdered sugar after baking. I peered out the window, watching the ground be covered in whiteness, hovering between feeling the joy and novelty of this experience and the sadness of a foreigner.

Winter was coming and we only had three weeks left until the end of the semester. I rushed to fulfill my academic commitments, I rushed to classrooms, the library, the cafeteria, Prince House; I read in a rush, wrote in a rush, and tried to figure out by phone what would be required for me to buy a ticket home, even if it cost me all I had. At the time, even though I had requested to defer the remainder of my university fees balance, I had less than four hundred dollars to my name. I would travel, that I had decided, even if I had to borrow money.

This is the state I was in when I left Amherst for Boston one bitingly cold winter morning with one of my colleagues. Less than two hours after setting off, we arrived.

My colleague dropped me off in one of the central squares after describing how to get to the airline office in the Statler Hilton hotel. This was the first time I'd left Amherst since arriving three months previously. Now that I was walking around in the hubbub of big city crowds, the town seemed like a tiny, remote mountain village. Little houses painted in white with brick roofs, two intersecting main streets that passed by the church, the police station, the firehouse, the coffee shop, the Lord Jeffrey Inn, the flower shop, the funeral home, the bookstores, and a few other shops. It was a placid town that had its own distinctive bustle, because it was mostly full of students. Amherst College was located at the intersection of the two main streets; to the north lay the University of Massachusetts and there were three more colleges only a few miles away.

I pushed the hotel's glass door open and entered the busy, elegant lobby with its wealthy guests milling about. I asked about the Olympic Airlines office and found it. A half hour later, I left, a Boston–Athens round-trip ticket in my purse. The company had reduced the fares during the Christmas holidays so that Greeks living abroad could go home to visit their families. I pushed the glass door open once again and exited. I was as happy as a child leaving a shop who'd been able to buy the very toy she'd dreamed of. I had a ticket in my purse that had cost three hundred dollars; the plane would leave Boston on the twenty-third of December and return four weeks later. I couldn't have arranged anything better. I would write to Mourid so he could send me a ticket to travel from Athens to Cairo. I had less than a hundred dollars left. This would have to be enough to cover all of my expenses until then and also to buy a few presents.

I then went to the Greek consulate to get a visa. When I'd finished, it was almost two o'clock in the afternoon. My plan to get to know the city's landmarks or visit some of the museums started to seem impossible, because I wanted to get back to Amherst before evening. I ate a quick lunch then went to wander through the streets, where people were looking around, peering through shop windows, and staring up at the skyscrapers. Then I went to the central bus terminal in Park Square and bought a ticket. I went into the station's coffee shop to have a cup of coffee. Why did everyone here look so miserable? Most of the people sitting in the coffee shop were dressed modestly, and their faces had the premature wrinkles that distinguish people who have worked hard all their lives. I left the station and walked around the neighborhood, waiting for my bus to leave. There was a big shop near the station that had funny burlesque pictures and statues in its large glass window displays. My curiosity propelled me to go in. The shopkeeper asked me, "What can I do for you?"

"Thanks, I'm just having a look."

The man's resentful gaze embarrassed me so I went back outside. I walked for several minutes before I realized that the streets seemed deserted. Wasn't that strange at this time of day? It seemed like this street was full of shops, so I carried on. There was a row of little shops whose windows were packed with nude photos of people in both common and unusual sexual positions, and small entryways whose signs announced that they were showing erotic films. I realized that perhaps this street was a part of the city's red-light district and felt a bit anxious about being all alone. Was this because of a fear instilled in all of us as children that makes us believe the female body is threatening and should be feared? Was it my awareness as a woman of being reluctant to allow men's lust-filled eyes to intrude upon my body? Or was it the anxiety of a foreign woman in a place whose customs she simply doesn't know? I walked back to the bus station and immediately understood why the shopkeeper had looked at me like that when I told him confidently and with the innocence of a country girl, "I'm just having a look!"

When the bus got underway to Amherst at five PM, I reclined my seat a little, rested my head, stretched my legs out in front of me, and closed my eyes. Oh, if only I were sitting in an airplane headed to Cairo!

Two days before my trip I had finished all of my required classes. One cold winter's morning, having only slept three hours the night before, I started going back over what I had written and finding typing errors which I corrected. Then I put all my work in two big brown envelopes with the professors' names on each. I left home, heading first to the English department to drop off one of them, and then to the Afro-American Studies department to drop off the other. I promised myself that after I got back home I would have a long sleep that even an alarm clock couldn't interrupt. But when I left the secretary's office I found myself bounding down the stairs with the energy of ten monkeys. Had I not just completed my first full semester of studies? Would I not be in Cairo in only four more days, five at the most?

I drank a cup of coffee and went back to Prince House, where I borrowed one of my housemates' bikes and decided to go down to the center of town and buy a few gifts. I passed by Prince House, pushing the bike next to me, and when I reached the end of the street I mounted and rode it. On the street sloping down the hill, it was as if the bicycle was enchanted, flying along the ground. I'd had a bike I liked to ride as a little girl, but when I reached adolescence, my father started objecting to me taking it out on the street. So for me, riding a bicycle remained tied to childhood innocence and automatic self-confidence, which gradually started eroding with the anxieties of the teenage years and increasing doubts about what I could really do. Since the bike flew like this with me on it, or I was flying with it, or the sloping hill was itself flying by with the two of us, my childish feelings of power, competence, and un-bridled joy in my existence returned. "Do I never manage to take the return trip into account?" I asked myself impatiently because I was forced to walk back on foot; riding the bike up the hill became impossible between the steep incline and the weight of the things I had bought. I hung the bags on the handlebars and carried a box in one hand, pushing the bike up the road with the other.

Two days later, I left Amherst with one of my colleagues who was also on his way to Boston. I had decided to spend the night there to be ready for my journey early the following morning. We left Amherst in the afternoon. The weather was relatively warm and rainy. The trip took us more than three hours because of flood-ing, and the continuous heavy rain meant that the cars on the road were enveloped in a dense fog. The rain beat monotonously against the car, its sounds mixing with the continual swish of the windshield wipers.

When we finally reached Boston it was evening, and there was no sign of rain—just a sharp, stormy wind. My colleague dropped me off at the hotel. I paid for my room up front and telephoned for a taxi to take me to the airport early in the morning. Then I put some coins into a vending machine, which gave me a hot cup of coffee with milk, a piece of cake, and a pack of cigarettes. I went up to my room.

The next morning, I went to Logan Airport and took a short domestic flight to New York's Kennedy Airport. I waited many hours until six that evening for the flight to Athens. I walked around the huge airport; it was as big as a small city. I browsed in some of the book and magazine stalls and had lunch in one of the fast-food restaurants. Then I searched for a place to sit that wasn't especially noisy.

I sat and smoked, then leaned my head back on the chair, stretching my legs out in front of me. They wouldn't call the passengers for my flight for at least another hour and a half, perhaps more. In the seat across from me was a stocky woman with deep red-brown colored skin, like someone from Upper Egypt. Her face had those particular lines on them from an earlier time. She had the face of someone who'd labored hard and her hands revealed this as well. Why did this woman look so Egyptian? I felt an urge to go up to her and ask her if she saw me sitting across from her. Aren't you from my country, Spanish-speaking woman? I continued staring at her and learned that she was from Puerto Rico. Everything about her told me this—her face, her language, the fullness of her hips, and her presence that had labored under American colonialism. No doubt she was returning to her island. Was it for some occasion, I wondered? Or for a visit to her family and country, having saved up money for years? The woman got up from her seat. Had they announced her flight? She walked relatively slowly, and I closed my eyes and saw another woman. Was it the resemblance between them that struck me, carried over from an image that lingered in my mind? The woman from my memory was around fifty years old, from one of the villages in the Delta. She also had that pure, deeply hued red-brown skin and jet-black hair, of which you could see only a wisp when it escaped from under the tassels on her headscarf. Her eyebrows were perfectly arched, like rising half-moons; she had dark blue, Arab-style kohl around her eyes and a green tattoo under her lower lip. I thought Um Fathy was so beautiful and always had a lovely scent. Why was I remembering her now, sitting in the airport with my eyes half closed in a departure hall full of travelers at JFK Airport?

I picked up my handbag and walked toward the little jet bridge connecting the building to the airplane door. I finally sat down but I couldn't recline my seat or stretch my legs. I just sat calmly and fastened my seatbelt, waiting for takeoff.

The journey was long, and the plane flew for ten full hours. Winter journeys are annoying because air pockets cause turbulence and each time the plane would plunge it seemed like we were going to go down. My stomach was continuously upset by the sudden, unexpected jolts. My exhaustion and lack of sleep made me feel even more constricted, so I felt as if I were suffocating in the darkness that gave other passengers a good night's sleep. I turned on the little light above my head but this felt even more suffocating.

Then we started entering dawn; only a bit of purplish-blue was left in the sky, leading to a day that mixed pomegranate red, lemon yellow, and orange. The Greek woman sitting next to me who'd slept the entire journey came to life suddenly, looked out the window, and started talking to me and to herself. She also talked to the people sitting in front of us and behind us. She punctuated everything she said by repeating, "Greece is so amazing!" The view out the window truly was amazing; this was not only true in the eyes of a woman going back to her country after being abroad. The islands were flooded by the glow of the sun, as though the country were made of gold or as if the sea were the sun. Did ancient Greeks see their country in this way from atop a mountain? Did it seem to them that the young god Apollo with the flowing tresses came to them on a chariot of gold? Nothing could have drawn me away from this scene except the sudden loud hubbub of the passengers on the plane. All of them save two or three were Greeks going back to spend the holiday in their country. At night the plane had been silent. Everyone was sleeping or quiet because they were dreaming or afraid. When the plane began to fly over Greece, not one of them stayed seated. They all started talking loudly, and singing as the plane prepared to land. The flight attendants repeated their request that the passengers be seated and fasten their seatbelts. It was as if they were asking people in the midst of a celebration to tame their spirits!

When the wheels touched down at the airport, the passengers burst into applause and words of thanks for the pilot. Though the flight attendants announced that people should stay seated, everyone started unfastening their seatbelts and getting out of their seats. I got off the plane, feeling weak and fragile. Was it exhaustion from a sleepless night, or the bright light of the islands and the brilliance of people in their presence? Perhaps I was just worn out from my long journey. Or perhaps returning to Egypt was more than my heart could handle.

A taxi took my suitcases and me to a modest hotel not too far from Parliament Square in the center of Athens. I had to wait until the morning of the following day until I could figure out my trip to Cairo. I wanted to have a shower but there was only cold water. I washed my face, hands, and feet and then fell asleep. Later I went out on a tourist trip around the city. Then I came back and fell asleep again.

When I went out the next day, the shops were still closed. Even most of the cafés I passed were closed. The hotel I was staying in didn't have a restaurant and I wanted to have breakfast. I found a place to have a cup of tea and two slices of bread with cheese. Surely airline offices didn't open before eight in the morning. I finished my breakfast and it still wasn't even seven thirty AM. I walked in the streets, looking around and waiting. I started with Egyptair, but the office was still closed. I went to other companies—Olympian Airlines, Air France, Alitalia, none of which I had a ticket for. It seemed most likely that Mourid would have sent me a ticket on Egyptair. Finally, I went back to the office at nine thirty and found it open. I asked if there was a ticket waiting for me, in the name of Radwa Ashour. The woman started flipping through all the telegrams she had received and replied, "No."

"Are you sure?"

"I'm sure."

I left the Egyptair office, my annoyance mixed with confusion, concern, and anxiety. I hoped Mourid was OK. Perhaps my telegram hadn't reached him. What would I do then? Would I have enough money to buy a one-way ticket to Cairo? I had to calculate the cost of the hotel and the taxi to get me to the airport. I really hoped that Mourid was fine. I thought I should sit down in a café to calmly plan my next steps. On the way, I spotted a sign for Suez Air—I'd missed their office the first time. I went in and asked a handsome young man in a dark blue steward's uniform. He told me, "There's no ticket here in your name. Who knows… perhaps the telegram you sent to Cairo never arrived."

He was quiet for a moment and then said, "I can send a telegram by telex to our office in Cairo and they can call the person who will pay the cost of your ticket on the telephone. Then you can phone Cairo and follow up."

The young man described a place where I could make an international phone call. I asked him, "Should I come back to your office afterwards or call you?"

"It's ten AM now, and our flight to Cairo takes off at five PM. Go to the airport before three PM. If the response has come they will give you your ticket there and you will fly out straight away. We have seats."

The young man was very friendly. I thanked him and went to
the telephone office where I called the friends of ours in Cairo to
ask them to inform Mourid about the ticket situation. I learned
that my telegram hadn't reached him and that he'd been anxious
he'd had no news of me.

While paying my bill for the one night I'd spent at the hotel,
I told the person at the desk, "Don't be surprised if I come back
again with my suitcase in a couple of hours!" and I laughed.

But my heart was heavy, and so was my suitcase. I walked to
the intersection to get a taxi more easily.

That evening everyone was celebrating Christmas. The streets
were crowded and noisy and there weren't many taxis. Perhaps I
would arrive home tonight, returning to familiar faces and voices,
or perhaps I would spend it here on a cold, lonely street looking through the many closed shop windows without celebrating
the holiday. I would simply head back to my cold room at the
hotel, waiting there in annoyance under the dim, lemony glow of
the lamp. I swallowed the lump in my throat and my stream of
gloominess along with it. Why anticipate problems? I asked the
taxi driver who was moving at a worrying speed how long the trip
to the airport took.

The young man who worked at the Suez Air branch office was
now at the counter in the airport. He wrote out the ticket and then
gave it to me. I looked at him joyfully, with love; at that moment
he was like someone in ancient Greece delivering sudden, happy
news to the people of the city. I thanked him as he handed me
my ticket. Then I went to check my luggage and get my passport
stamped. The announcement that the plane had been delayed by
two hours didn't make me miserable. I would be in Cairo that
night. Suddenly, it was a holiday! A woman doesn't just laugh
for no reason, or dance in the middle of an airport crowded with
travelers if she hasn't lost her mind. I actually was still sane, but I
was laughing and wanted to dance and shout out my happiness. I
sat down to get a bite to eat and drink a cup of coffee. I found it

difficult to stay seated, however, and calmly swallow my food. I got back up to walk around the airport and bought a little brown clay jug decorated with black lines and triangles. It was really pretty and would go well in Mourid's office, as a pen holder. Greetings, you Greek artisans, you Greeks who I only spent a few heavy-hearted hours with—greetings and until we meet again!

I was aware that the journey was almost over when the flight attendant brought around a basket with clean, warm cotton towels. She smiled as she handed me one to wipe my hands and face with. I went to the washroom to fix myself up before the plane started its descent. "I wonder how I will look to everyone after these months of being away?" I asked myself, standing in front of the mirror hanging above the metal sink in the plane's washroom. I was a little bit thinner and my hair was still short—it didn't even cover my ears. Why were my cheeks so rosy? Actually, they weren't so much rosy as red. I hope I'm not sick, I thought. I put kohl around my eyes, brushed my hair, and went back to my seat.

I fastened my seatbelt and the plane started preparing to land. From afar Cairo looked like an impossible city, lone clusters of light in the middle of a sea of desert darkness. I couldn't see the city from the plane at all, at night. I became two people: one strapped into an airplane seat flying in the sky over the city, and the other fixed in the ground like a tree trunk or a stone in a wall. My eyes were looking through the little glass window while flying through the darkness and light, searching for the Nile, which I couldn't see even though I knew it was there. The plane approached the airport runway and when the wheels hit the ground it pushed forward with sudden speed. Then finally it stopped. I got up out of my seat and put my jacket on calmly, as if the door of the plane would not open just a moment later, and as if the iron customs barrier wouldn't lead out to the city and my loved ones. I walked calmly with everyone else toward the airplane door… as if my heart were still inside me.

Chapter Five

The same road, the same slow pace. I sat in the shrunken darkness, staring at the regular motion of the wipers on the bus's big glass windscreen. Heavy rain on an ancient night. The only people left on the bus were the driver and me. The rain was not stopping. The journey that had started to seem like an endless punishment, however, was almost at an end. I got out of my seat and went up to the driver to ask, "As you can see, it's gotten late and the weather is terrible. When you pass by the next street could you please let me off in front of the student residence?"

"I only stop at the scheduled stops!"

It didn't even cross my mind that the driver would refuse my request. But he passed right in front of the student residence, drove all the way alongside it and then turned right down another road. He didn't even slow down until he'd reached the next stop. He got off the bus and opened the luggage compartment in the belly of the bus. He handed me my suitcase without either one of us opening our mouths, as if in a silent movie, then got back on the bus and drove off.

Indeed, the impossible had happened. I carried my suitcase in one hand and my carry-on bag in the other and started walking very carefully. The ground was covered with a thin layer of ice, the cold air making the rain freeze. I was afraid of putting my foot down wrong, slipping, and falling down onto my back. It was almost one in the morning. I walked a few steps and then stopped, resting my suitcase on the ground for a few seconds before continuing.

On the bus from Boston, my misery was all consuming. I was completely shattered after a long day of travel that I had begun before six in the morning, waiting for a car that would take me and other passengers from the Olympic Airways office in Athens to the airport. The plane took off at nine in the morning and we arrived in New York after more than ten hours in the air. The plane landed late and I had to run to get my bag and transfer to another terminal to catch the plane to Boston. That plane took off and landed. I took a taxi from the airport to the central bus station where I caught the last bus leaving for Amherst.

I arrived at the back door of Prince House at long last. I took my key out of my purse, opened the door, and went in. I climbed the stairs to my room on the second floor. I noticed that the walls were a depressing mix of cement, sand, and little gray stones. Strange I never noticed how depressing these walls were before! I thought while walking down the long corridor to my room. But as I turned the key in the lock, I thought, at least it's warm here and there's a rug on the floor. I don't have to be afraid of suddenly falling and breaking an arm or a leg.

But as soon as I turned on the light and looked at my room, I realized that my visit to Cairo was over, and I had to put it behind me so I could advance down a path in the opposite direction… at least for the long months ahead. "I have to sleep now!" I said, looking through the messages that a friend of mine had picked up and stacked neatly on my desk before she traveled to spend the holiday with her family. "I have to sleep now…" I repeated to myself, seeing that it was now past two AM. The air in the room felt suffocating. I opened the window. "Maybe my colleague is back already from the holiday." I sat on my bed without changing my clothes and thought once again about how my address had become: Room 224, Prince House, University of Massachusetts.

I emptied my suitcase into my drawers, thinking that the travel cycle was finished. I'd gone and come back. Now I was simply faced with a new beginning. I took out two cotton shawls, one orange, the other blue. As I was folding them I thought to myself: the orange one is for Susy and the blue one is for Anna. I put them in one of my drawers. As soon as I closed it, the scent of incense wafted up. I'd bought these scarves in Khan al-Khalili a few days before my journey. I opened the drawer again and bent over to inhale their fragrance. I was confused and I couldn't tell if the scent was in my nose or in the scarves. Why does the slender minaret of the Hussein mosque surprise me every time I see it, as if I'd never seen it before? Why does the same urge to cry overtake me every time I glimpse the cornices and minarets of al-Azhar in my imagination? Is it because I feel I am denied its history? I sat on the edge of my bed; students at al-Azhar sit among its pillars—on the ground surrounding their teacher, listening to him. They fill buckets with water to moisten the parched ground. I remain trapped by the feminine "a" at the end of my name; I am a person who can only walk barefooted on the carpets of this time-less mosque as a visitor and stranger. I can't lean my back against the marble pillars in the courtyard, and I can't spend a summer's afternoon in its shade, contemplating the possible and impossible. I'm not called on with other supporters of the leader's victory in war or of the fall of tyrannical leaders. I thought, this millennium is a history I don't have access to.

I got up to open the door to my room. One of my housemates had come to say hi to me. When she left I went back to unpacking my suitcase and putting things in drawers. When I finished, I closed the suitcase and put it under my bed. Now I had to send my film to be developed. I took three envelopes and wrote the name of the office where they develop photographs on them. After a week or ten days at the most, the pictures came back developed. They were pictures of me and Mourid and our friends—pictures of us sitting next to the Nile, crossing the street, sitting at home. There were pictures I took in Athens on the steps of the Dionysian Theater at the Acropolis and the lush green grass sprouting from in between the stones on the floors of the ancient temples. There were pictures of the sun setting over the columns of the Temple of Poseidon, god of the sea in Sounion, where the Aegean Sea meets the Mediterranean. What would those moments look like fixed still in photographs?

I still had the little camera, smaller than my hand, with me. I started taking pictures to capture different scenes with a childish joy. This was not only because the camera was new but also because I was happy and relished this chance. Despite this, I didn't dare photograph any of the spoils of war—the tanks and rockets left behind by the Israelis east of the canal, on display in Gezira. The army built a miniature version of the Bar Lev line where a young, dark-skinned soldier explained to the Egyptian troops the way to storm the Israeli barricade.

The tanks shone brilliantly in the bright light of day. Dozens of children in vibrantly colored clothes were climbing all over them and playing noisily. The tanks were like colorful, decorated swings put up for the holidays, like the paper ribbons people hang up in popular areas on feast days. The celebratory atmosphere was touching enough to make you smile. This is the inheritance of grief and joy: empty, hollow men pin medals on themselves and barter the blood of soldiers and the history of the country for mere handfuls of straw to shore up their own waning strength. A friend of mine said, "Save some of your bitterness for later, there's more yet to come!"

Mourid kept all the newspapers published during these times for me. There were dozens that he'd saved that hadn't reached Amherst. I'd only seen two editions of Al-Ahram, more than a month after they'd been published. I'd read them in the library. In normal circumstances the library received them regularly. It was evening and the library was lit by neon lights as I apprehensively read transcriptions of Sadat's speeches. When I finished reading the papers, a powerful feeling of fear seized me. I got up from my seat, headed for the library exit, and walked outside. I heard a voice repeating my name. It was one of my Egyptian colleagues, rushing over to me, "Are you OK? Are you ill?"

"I was reading Al-Ahram. He said, 'They took 10 kilometers from me.'"

"Who said that?"

"Sadat. I was reading his speech. He is talking about land as if it was his alone to do what he wants to with it."

My friend invited me for a cup of coffee but I made an excuse not to go. I wanted to go back to my room and be alone to try to understand if what I had read was really so frightening or if being abroad exaggerated things.

It wasn't just being far from home. Mourid told me, "Since Sadat made his speech on the sixteenth of October, when they announced the ceasefire and preparations for negotiations, the meaning of this war became clear, as did the context in which he took the decision to fight it. When we were watching him give the speech on television here, I told my friends that I could smell a rat. They said that I was too quick to react, that I always exaggerate everything. Then on the eighteenth of October, I met a writer friend of mine and he started off asking, 'Isn't it wonderful what happened, Mourid?' I told him, 'It's frightening!' He replied, 'Don't be the bearer of bad news' and I told him, 'I think he is getting what he deserves, and so be it. And I am the bearer of bad news.'"

I put on my coat and left Prince House. I breathed the cold air with a heavy heart and troubled mind. I walked through the barren winter streets, their snow banks piled high on either side, all the way to the town hall. I went in the first café I passed and sat down on one of the tall stools, resting my arms against the long wooden bar underneath it. I asked the waitress for a cup of coffee and searched my pockets—perhaps I'd find a long-forgotten painkiller inside them. I stared at the metal ring on my finger in front of me. I'd bought it at the fair that sold war booty. They told us that it was from the wreckage of Israeli airplanes. I contemplated it resting on my left hand next to my wedding ring, while waiting for my cup of American coffee.

Two days after I arrived, most students started coming back to get ready for the spring academic semester that stretched from the beginning of February to the end of May. The noise of students had returned to a campus that only two days before had been desolate and extremely cold. On the day of course registration, the place was awake, lively, and longing for joy. Was this liveliness because of the huge number of young people chatting, laughing, and strolling around? Was it the joy of friends meeting? Or are new beginnings always like this? Students came and went throughout the campus and the foyers of buildings. A huge number of them were crowded into the building where registration was held. They were standing in long lines, waiting their turn.

I registered again for four courses this semester—two in Afro-American Literature, one in Nigerian Literature, and one in Theories of Romance Literature. I filled out the forms, handed them in, and then headed for the building where the required books were sold. I took the books I needed and some others that I couldn't resist the temptation to buy. I then stood in line and waited for my turn to pay. The books were lined up on wooden shelves and stacked up on the floor; each stack had a sign with the name of the department and course number on it. This took me back to the place that sold books in the school I'd studied in as a girl. On the ground floor was a large area, forbidden for us to enter, that was full of new books, notebooks, pens, and all kinds of colors. We stood at the threshold of this impossible, magical cavern, glimpsing some of its treasures through the iron bars over its windows. And then we would ask to buy this or that book. Every year before classes started, our parents would wait with us in the long line on the ground floor, in front of the wooden beam blocking the door of the place where they would buy our required books. My father would pay for them. I would come home happy, my leather school bag bursting with books that all had that special new-book smell.

At first it was the pictures that appealed to me. Then through the years there would be fewer and fewer pictures and I started to get used to unlocking the symbolism behind the words in them. But always, whether there were pictures or not, I liked the smell of new books, when their scent wafted up to me as I turned the pages or put my nose near them. Old books also have a pungent smell, mixing with bits of dust, filling my nose while I am doing research in the relative darkness of the overloaded stacks at the Ain al-Shams University library, the Cairo University library, or here. But this scent is different—I love it and how it penetrates my nose and lungs. I put the required books that I'd bought into two big brown paper bags, and then went out into the street.

At home, I was still looking through my new books that I was happy to own when there was a knock on my door. One of my Puerto Rican friends entered in that noisy Latin way of hers that I loved, and said bossily, "Don't eat dinner tonight, because we are going to eat for free!"

I told her jokingly, "Does this mean that you discovered a shelter that feeds students?"

"The university cafeteria is open from today on, but the monitors aren't asking anyone for their membership cards yet because the administration didn't realize how many cards it had to make. We don't have a membership, but we'll go and eat a meal for free. We have a date at five."

At five o'clock, we headed down from Prince House to the cafeteria nearest to us. We were ten students from six different countries, who had been united by living far from home. We'd all become friends. We decided to invite ourselves to dinner on the university administration. The idea of eating for free in the United States, where everything cost money, stirred up huge excitement and a generally childish glee in us. One of our friends said, "I told Theresa, the Polish girl, to come with us, and she was really surprised. She told me it wasn't right to do this. 'This is stealing,' she said, can you believe it?" Theresa's shock at what we were all doing was no less than everyone's shock at Theresa's reaction.

We stood in line, each of us waiting our turn in this long procession of students. Then we took our food and sat together around a table big enough for all of us. During the previous semester I had eaten two meals a day in the university cafeteria, except on Saturdays and Sundays. After more than three months of eating like this I couldn't stand to go there. Sitting alone while eating depressed me, as though I were someone condemned to being always alone. The excessive amounts of food and the amount that was left over and just thrown away in the trash outraged me. But when I was sitting among my friends, I was happy, loud, and enjoyed myself. It was as if by sitting all together like this, there was an automatic promise of synergy. All of us were lonely and far from home. We needed this. None of us said any of this aloud, but we all picked up on this promise and clung onto it tenaciously.

After this dinner, we started having group dinner parties in one of the study rooms in Prince House every two to three weeks, or whenever there was an occasion. We would push all the desks together and they would become a long table like at a wedding. We would lay out the paper plates, cups, and napkins, the plastic spoons, forks, and knives, a flower here and there. Then the person who had invited everyone would come in surrounded by friends, carrying the still-hot trays of food from the kitchen. This little parade would be greeted with happiness and cheering. This food cooked in banana leaves, or white Puerto Rican rum mixed with coconut water and pineapple juice, was a geography summoning us. We would try it as friends and finish together. I—who never liked cooking—made okra with meat and tomatoes and prepared Arab sweets with the pride of a grandmother preparing them for her grandchildren. When I carried them in to place them on the table made of desks, I knew that I was offering both them and myself, far from home, a way for us all to inhabit a piece of my faraway country.

Chapter Six

It was the beginning of March and Mourid was writing from Cairo about the merging of spring into summer. Here I woke up in the morning and watched the soft snowflakes on the ground, which was still white. I observed this from behind the window of my room and surprised myself by enjoying the scene. I washed my face, drank my coffee, and put on my coat to go out. I now knew and was used to this huge area with so many buildings that had seemed like a labyrinth when I arrived, and which I had to navigate with Ariadne's legendary string. This included both the modern buildings next to each other on the southwest side of campus, that were called the towers because they were so tall, in which thousands of students lived, to the student residences on the northeast side, that had brick ceilings and weren't more than four stories tall. Between the two of them were the university's many buildings, which were constructed over a period of ten years when it was being established in the middle of the nineteenth century.

When I got to the university at the end of the summer, the lake in the center of campus was like something imaginary from a fairy tale. Its shimmering surface reflected the image of its swimming swans, the trees around it, the little church with its brick roof and steeple. But in the middle of winter the lake only reflected whiteness. Snow covered the stone church, its roof, and its bell tower. Green ivy fell from its dark gray walls, with only a few dry branches still wrapped around its ancient stones. The church and South College facing it were both built with the same kind of local stone. The nearby library, in contrast, was the most modern building on campus.

This tall building ruined the specificity of the place like an architecturally modern, erect coffin. Its sixteen stories are incompatible with its surroundings. One of my girlfriends said with wicked sarcasm, "The architect sure had a penchant for masculine symbols!"

Smiling, I replied, "It's the American penchant for everything being superlative. It's exactly like the signs at the bottom of the Empire State Building in New York—'This building is taller than that one, bigger than that one, it has more floors than that one.' Surely they don't need a sixteen-story library but they needed to say that we have the tallest library in the region, or the northeast of the country, or in the whole country!"

It was a truly awful building whose towering height caused a wind tunnel that could be very bothersome for those walking by it. Inside the library there were many facilities, including a huge number of books, periodicals, and reference works, as well as coin-operated photocopy machines. It was also easy to get materials they didn't have from other university libraries, or public libraries, through a special loan division. They would request material for a certain period of time or have a copy of it made for you.

Waiting for the elevator to take me down to the ground floor, I wondered what kind of unjust time we are living in that makes us compare this stone coffin to that ancient other one, like an age-old tree trunk whose dinginess contains a roughness that we sap of life? I see a building with Islamic architecture, looming over me, near Bab al-Khalq Square in Cairo. I smell its distinctive damp scent and corroded stairs. Neon lights illuminate its corridors morning and night. I see its copies of the Qur'an, open to gold-lettered pages, on display in the long hallway where the card catalog was located. I remember the washroom with its peeling paint, which whenever I went in I changed my mind about using it. I could never shake off its foul smell. I gave my card to the American

man responsible for lending me the books I wanted and he finished everything in two minutes on the little electronic screen.
He gave me the books. His speed only reminded me more of the
trouble of waiting so long for the book I needed, the painstaking
searching on the library's bookshelves, which hadn't been dusted
in months, and the terrible, confusing catalogs. I pushed open the
library doors and headed to my room in Prince House, one thing
repeating over and over again in my mind: What unjust times... I
passed the lake, the little church, and the administration building
and then stopped suddenly, saying to myself, "Whether we did
justice to our times or they were unjust to us is not the issue. The
important thing is that we carried on through difficult times!"

I put the books down in my room, and then went back outside
to walk down the same road passing by the administration building, the little church, the lake, and the library. I planned to have a
quick lunch in the campus center so that I could be at the English
department before two o'clock, to attend my literary theory class.
The thin old American man had proposed the first time we all met
together—him and the five students registered in the course—
that we move our weekly meetings to his house, a calmer and more
intimate setting. Therefore, each week we would meet up in the
department and then go together in three cars, the professor's and
those of two students, through the winding mountain roads that
led out of the village to his house. He had prepared everything
for us to sit comfortably: antique chairs, a wood-burning stove
that gave an exceptional warmth to the little room, a big electric
kettle to make coffee, paper cups, and little packets of sugar. The
professor sat by himself on the sofa, his books and papers placed
on a rectangular table in front of him. He would start speaking in
a low, calm voice, linking, comparing, and raising questions. This
man was truly well-versed in his area of specialization. However, it
is also true that everything made this feel like time for a siesta: the
snow outside and the warmth inside, the cozy room, the hot coffee
after lunch, the absolute silence save the crackling of wood in the

fireplace and the boiling kettle. I tried in vain to follow what he was saying all the way to the end, but I was unsuccessful—his voice not only didn't stop me from wanting to fall asleep, but actually made me want to even more. When I succeeded in overcoming my sleepiness, I was still unable to concentrate on what the professor was saying. I would follow one idea and then that idea would carry me down another path, different from what he would be talking about afterwards.

He was talking about what Coleridge took from German Idealism and I was reciting passages from the "Rime of the Ancient Mariner." I listened attentively to what he was saying at first about the gaps in Shelley's critical theory, and my mind wandered off to think about the critical issues that concerned me. I endeavored to come up with my own definition of the nature of poetry and its function. One day, I almost laughed out loud when I looked over at my colleague sitting in front of me and saw her half-asleep. Another colleague sitting on the chair next to her was fighting off yawns. I remembered naptime in kindergarten when the teacher used to tell us to fold our arms on our desks and put our heads down on them. I started calling these afternoons "required nap-time" for doctoral students! To be honest, there was only one time when I had no desire at all to sleep in this class, stretching from two to five in the afternoon—when it was my turn to give a long presentation on the critical theories of German Idealist writers.

But Julius Lester's lecture[1] was something completely differ-ent. Though it was early in the morning, I went even before I had totally shaken off the sleepy film covering my eyes. Julius was a small, thin man in his thirties. He had brown skin and kinky, short black hair. He wore a small earring that he never took off. As soon as he entered the room, he took off his coat and started talking

---

1   Julius Lester was a prominent member of the Student Non-Violent Coordinating Committee (SNCC), one of the organizations that played a fundamental role in the Black freedom movement of the sixties. He is a political writer, academic, and researcher in Black popular heritage as well as a singer and composer, who has many books and recordings to his name.

until all of the students were swept away by his sonorous voice and the rhythm of his phrases. He carried them on his wings, flying them high like a giant bird, who soared and followed through in the flow, turned unexpectedly and then plunged as if he were about to fall, suddenly rising up again. The eyes of his listeners revealed the thrill of this adventure, in the presence of the bird who stood before us in the garb of a thin young man telling the tale of his enslaved people in a way that we would forever remember in detail. When the bird began speaking, he couldn't bear to have his shoes on, so he would bend down, take them off, and put them to the side. He did this every time. Then he would continue talking.

I really appreciated this man. I was drawn to what he could do and wanted to get closer to him, but the birdman didn't spread his wings in this same way in the street. In fact, he shrunk down strangely when he walked—alienated, distracted, and alone. In his office in the Afro-American Studies department, he met students by appointment to give them support. Sometimes he brought his young son whom he was looking after, and who'd sit on the rug in the office with coloring books and a pile of markers while his father was hunched over the books and papers on his desk.

The seven o'clock evening news on television reported that the phenomenon of group streaking had started spreading at universities—students at the University of North Carolina had achieved a record number when more than three hundred male and female students ran around together totally naked at one time. News reports are for people to listen to, process, and be affected by. So not even one day had passed when announcements were hung all over the university that South West, the largest student residence on campus, and Prince House as well, had decided to hold a streaking party. This meant the participants getting naked together, setting off at eleven o'clock at night from their meeting point in South West, running together naked to the university campus center, going inside, and then returning. The news excited everyone on campus, both those who wanted to participate and those who wanted to watch. As for my group of friends, all of whom were foreign observers of this American scene, we laughed like old folks making fun of young people at a wedding. We thought, "Why don't we also have our own little party at that time? We can eat, drink, and dance in the classroom that looks out over the South West towers and then when it's time for the event we can look out the window, and participate by watching!"

When I saw my two Iranian friends armed with cameras, I remarked jokingly: "I see that you are going to take some improper photos!" One of them responded with a laugh, "Indeed! Photographs witness a place and a time."

"Actually, what bothers me the most about these young people being naked for no understandable reason is that they will be exposed to the bitter cold. And tomorrow they will probably all wake up with pneumonia!"

We didn't discuss it any further and went back to our talking and chatting about other topics, putting aside the main event of the evening until we had almost totally forgotten it.

"They've started to appear!" I don't know who was looking out the window like a control tower operator and gave us the alert, but we circled around to see a huge procession of students, completely naked except for their shoes, jogging from behind the back entrance of Prince House. I wondered if they were jogging because they felt so cold or because they were embarrassed by such an unfamiliar feeling of nakedness. I had never seen anything at all like this, ever. I said, "We should have gone down and looked at them close up."

Our German friend said, "But it's really cold!" Laughingly, I responded to him, "You've hardly missed anything—if you get ready, you can go down now and run behind them!"

We kept staring at them through the window, commenting on what was happening. Soon Mary and Sheila, who lived on the same floor, came in, boisterous and noisy. Mary said in her loud, husky voice, "What a sight! We put on our coats, went down, and waited for them to come out. We saw them passing by right in front of us!" She laughed with a mixture of nervous emotion and happiness.

"We took pictures of them! Their bodies were all shivering because it's so cold. Poor things. And the sight of the children... my God!"

She started chuckling. Sheila was talking to another group about how many streakers she estimated were there. It was clear there were hundreds of them. Sheila said confidently, "No less than four hundred!"

The next day, I was sitting in the English Department with the literary theory professor and one of my colleagues, waiting for the rest of the group so we could go to the professor's house for class. The university newspaper had published a report saying that there were nearly four hundred students. On the front page, they published a picture of a group of naked women streaking. Smiling calmly, the professor said, "A new craze." I said to myself, What drives these new crazes?

The answer was clear in the next day's edition of the *Daily Collegian*, when a representative from the Amherst Police Department, within whose jurisdiction the university falls, was questioned. He replied, "Why should we be worried? The students are enjoying themselves... This is healthy and it is definitely better than that political mania which obsessed them in the sixties."

The police wanted the students to enjoy themselves in this way en masse because their behavior served a common purpose, whereas when an individual acts out of the ordinary it doesn't accomplish anything at all. Just two days later the police arrested a student who ran through the university naked in broad daylight. They took him in, gave him a warning, and then released him.

Chapter Seven

What happens when suddenly the sound of chirping birds rises in the sky, an omen belying the stinging cold and bare trees, announcing that spring has come? Before I've even gotten out of bed, I think that I should greet the morning through my big glass windowpane during every season, so as to capture time. I wonder if these windows are bows and arrows, prison gates, or if we can even choose? Death resides in the shadow of prison gates: the battle is difficult and my eyes don't lie.

Frightened, the small woman walks ahead in Cairo as the boy Omar asks his mother with a piercing gaze, "Why is she so silent and her eyes so different?" As if I were merely a stone. The warbling of birds can make a stiff body move, it can feed the soul's need to be absent. I look at the pictures I took during my last visit to Cairo. Then I prepare my morning coffee, wash, and get ready to go out.

When we were sitting together at the university coffee shop, my friend Anna asked me why I wanted to sit for my comprehensive examinations immediately after I'd finished my course work that summer. "Why are you always in such a hurry? It's like you're rushing to try and catch a train…"

"Do you want to go with me to the Count Basie concert next week? He's playing here at the university."

"I'll go with you, but you didn't answer me. I was saying that you're always running, like you're trying to catch a train."

"Or like I'm afraid that the train will overtake me, Anna!"

I decided to submit my three areas of concentration for the

comprehensive examination as quickly as I could so that if the English Department's graduate studies committee agreed on them, I could sit for my examination as soon as possible and then would have finished with half of my program. Once again I would be rushing frantically in order to achieve what I wanted. I had to complete some basic readings before I would be able to write proposals for these examination areas in a way I would be satisfied with, so I continued attending courses and writing the essays and research papers the professors assigned.

This is how I spent the second half of March and the entire month of April—moving back and forth between lecture halls and the university library. Day after day, I worked to distinguish between millions of interlocking letters in words crammed into lines that recurred repeatedly on pages, establishing a connection between things that were specific and others that were as vast as the sea. The idea of the wide-open sea appealed to me and I dove in to it, oscillating between the apprehension of being just a small woman and the confidence of someone competent. Whenever I plunged deep into the vastness of the sea before me, I was confounded by my sailing craft, its captain, and its divers. Then I would be struck by a vague feeling that the library's fluorescent lights, the fine dust mixed with the pages of old books, and the darkness of the bookshelves in the upper stacks were suffocating—the sixteen-story library building had the somber darkness of an underground cellar. Perhaps it was more of a maritime cemetery. So why did the bright sunshine surprise me when I left that day to have lunch? Why was I tearful and trembling when I left the Amherst library at sunset and heard the gentle strumming of a guitar? The sound wafted through the air and I noticed a young man sitting on a rock, facing the shimmering hills on the horizon. The sky was clear and the warm music was a response to the exceptional warmth of that radiant spring day and its brilliant sunshine. I took off my shoes and walked on the grass, the land beneath my bare feet making me feel calm and stable.

My visits to Boston were always fleeting and limited. Despite this, the city drew me in. I liked its brick-roofed buildings, green spaces, and the Museum of Fine Arts with its European impressionist paintings and the statue *Epic of the Indian*. But the city also has a river, and I confess that a river in the city earns it a place in my heart. Though I had been to the city often, I hadn't yet visited any of its universities, or even any of the historical sites linked to the American Revolution. When my incredibly tall German colleague asked me if I wanted to accompany him and his girlfriend Ella to spend two days in Boston, I accepted. It was spring, but the weather was cold. The snow had melted, revealing the grass on the ground. Trees had sprouted tiny hard buds on their branches that at any moment now would surprise us with their greenness. This was my first visit to the city as a tourist, and Ella took on the task of being our guide. She decided that we would spend our two days in the city seeing its historical sites, visiting Harvard University, and hanging around Harvard Square, the area around the university campus. Ella's schedule even involved deliberate and intentional hanging around! We would get a drink in one of the crowded little cafés students frequented, have an apple and milky coffee for breakfast at the Pewter Pot restaurant, because it was famous and historical. Then we would have dinner the next day at a Chinese restaurant that—according to Ella's information and her unwritten schedule—served delicious food and had a view of the Charles River in Cambridge.

We left Amherst at eight o'clock on Saturday morning and we got to Boston two hours later, trying to sort out where we would stay. When we'd finished with that, Ella proposed that we start with the Freedom Trail.

"What's the Freedom Trail, Ella?"

"It is a path where the most important heritage sites of the American Revolution are located."

I didn't know why the American Revolution had never captured my interest when we studied it in high school, though I love history and momentous events spark my imagination. I still don't know why today. I've retained dozens of details about the French revolution, like Shahrazad's sister eavesdropping on the tales of the *One Thousand and One Nights*: the violent fall of the Bastille, starving masses, a feeble-minded king, skilled orators, a queen sent to the guillotine, the rise of a Corsican with a broad forehead, Phrygian caps, tricolor cockades pinned to chests, a new calendar, and a fiery passion that blew like the Western Wind that the poet wrote about on the other side of the channel.[2] Why didn't the American Revolution speak to me at all? Why as a teenager did I find it such a burden to memorize dates and the number of boxes of tea that they threw in the ocean and how much money they were worth?

"Yes, let's go to the Freedom Trail, Ella!"

We walked along the path, which was marked by a painted white line and stretched from the heart of the city of Boston to the harbor where the events of the Boston Tea Party took place in 1773, passing by the site of the Boston Massacre, and the Old South Meeting house, a church used as a headquarters by the groups that led the revolution and the people who participated in it. I walked along the white line and wished instead that I was sitting calmly in a café, drinking a cup of hot coffee. Was it the biting cold or Ella's irritating, brassy voice that made me withdraw deep into myself?

I completely turned my back on this scene, after the white line led us to an empty bit of land where Ella announced, "Five people were killed here in skirmishes between the people and British soldiers in March 1770. This event is known as the Boston Massacre."

Only a few months had passed since the massacre in the Chilean national stadium in Santiago after Pinochet's military coup overthrew Allende's elected government. Five thousand people were crowded into the stadium, waiting for the slaughter that soon would ensue throughout the entire country. The role the United States played in these massacres is well known.

---

2   The English poet here is Shelley and his "Ode to the West Wind."

I wonder when representatives will visit the site of the massacre of thousands in Santiago, where they cut off the singer-guitarist Victor Jara's hands before murdering him, sooner or later?

Ella enthusiastically and untiringly moved her jaw up and down; her German boyfriend was equally dull. As my legs followed the two of them along the never-ending white line, I thought about never-ending massacres. I wondered how many more massacres we should anticipate. The Six-Day War had delivered us over to the massacre of thousands in June 1970, which quieted down and was lost from sight only with the Black September massacres. Before the year passed, we were still wearing our mourning clothes and hadn't yet gotten used to the absence of those missing when we were assaulted by the events of Jerash and a new defeat. I wondered how many more massacres we should expect, how many wars would we have to fight. How many of those of us who fight will die this way, like the prophet, just as Abdel Khaliq and Shafi did?

"I'm finished walking on this trail and I'm going to leave now," I said to the others.

I brought a small poster of Picasso's painting *Guernica* back from Boston and hung it across from my bed in Prince House. But a short time later when I went to the Museum of Modern Art in New York City where the original work is displayed, I learned that this small reproduction is incommensurate with the genius of the original work. In fact, it negates its genius, like a postcard negates the miraculous architecture of a cathedral printed on it. The canvas covers an entire wall and the walls surrounding it display the plans Picasso sketched as soon as he heard about the bombardment of the village. The wild woman recurs in every drawing. Is this woman the centerpiece of the picture, or do works of genius always have multiple centers? The amputated hand of the horseman resolutely holding onto a flower on the lower edge of the canvas—is this not another center? The woman carrying her murdered son on the far left of the painting responds in pain to the heart of it. This is the

Guernica that contains my concerns and my experiences. I held it in my heart and removed the little reproduction from my wall.

Spring had still not completely arrived in Amherst at the end of April. But then May came and the earth changed. The people of the town could enter warm, happy spaces with new green on the trees and the soft scent of lilacs wafting through the open windows. You could hardly smell it during the day but at night it filled the air.

When winter is long, snow piles up on the ground and trees grow bare as if there is no hope life will ever return to them. A sunny spring day is as joyful as the birth of a child in a house where everyone else is elderly.

Thus when the month of May arrived, the university campus was brilliant with light and the bustle of students who had started celebrating the arrival of warm weather and the incipient end of the academic year. Many of them started wearing fewer clothes. Some wore shorts and walked barefooted enjoying the dewy grass. Some professors went outside with students and held their class discussions sitting on the grass. The sound of instruments reached the passersby who'd grown used to hearing it in front of the old church, which was now a rehearsal hall for musical groups.

The place was lively and sparkling, as if preparing for a wedding. I found myself walking through campus responding to its joy. I took two lilac stalks back to my room and put them in an empty glass coffee pot, filled it up halfway with water and placed it on the windowsill. I left the door to my room open and sat down at my desk.

I'd nearly finished my research for the academic year and had started preparing for my first comprehensive examination. The Graduate Studies Committee had agreed on the proposals I had presented and the date of June 18 was fixed for the examination.

In my entire academic life, I'd never before feared exams nor had they ever determined my daily activities. But this time I was scared. I experienced a fear of failure every day. I had decided that when I passed I would submit my dissertation proposal, pack up the sources and references I needed, and tackle writing the first part in Cairo. I wouldn't return to Amherst until January of the following year, connecting the summer holiday to the Christmas holiday and being away for the fall semester when I wasn't required to attend classes. And if I failed? This question left me feeling all alone, like a little girl standing at the intersection of a busy street—miserable and fearful of the torrent of cars that won't allow her to cross the street to get home. She is paralyzed, her eyes filled with tears.

My roommate left to spend the summer holiday with her family. My feeling of isolation in my own room had already built, as my roommate was starting to make me tense with her tireless search for a husband, her excessive love of sleep, the electric blanket she used to stay warm, and her long telephone calls to her mother in another state to ask her, "I have a headache... what should I do?" Despite this, I missed her. Not just because I missed the malicious spectator sport of observing her, but because I did know what a good person she was—I liked her and was used to her being there.

Most of the other people who lived in Prince House left too. It was empty except for a small number of foreign students like me who were preparing for some kind of examination. After the graduation ceremony at the end of June, the campus seemed totally empty, deserted.

So I carried on with preparing for the examination by familiarizing myself with the most important work published in the three specialized fields that I would be asked about. I started reading in the library instead of my room, even if I didn't need to. I spent my days sitting and reading and when I was exhausted I would go for a walk to one of the university coffee shops and have a sweet or ride into the center of town on my roommate's bicycle that she'd lent me.

The road into the main street of Amherst was beautiful; everything was green and the gardens of little one- or two-story houses were adorned with red and yellow lilies. A tree standing at one of the curves in the road surprised me every time I saw it because I'd never seen leaves like it before. Where had this tree gotten its wine-red leaves? I cycled to the ice cream parlor to have an ice cream cone, and then got back to work.

I went to my examination on June 18, 1974. My professor, the chair of the supervisory committee of my dissertation, offered me a cup of coffee, smilingly saying to me, "You have no reason to be worried!" Only at that moment did I realize that I had indeed been worried. It was an oral examination and the committee was made up of five professors. They began their questioning and I responded. The examination ended three hours later and they asked me to wait outside.

I sat in the next room, overwhelmed by exhaustion. Was it anxiety? After a few minutes they came out of the room to inform me of the results, and tell me what they thought about me traveling to Cairo to write. Did I look as pale as I did in the photograph taken after I finished my MA thesis defense, in which I was standing in my black university robes while the chairman of the committee read out the results? In that picture I look small and thin, like a teenage girl whose wide eyes expressed both intelligence and anxiety.

The older man, Professor Brogan, came out of the room first, smiling and telling me he had read my MA thesis and that he thought it was excellent. I was waiting for him to say something about the examination that day. Did he have nothing to say except to praise my old work? I was wrong, though. The chair of the committee was supposed to announce the result. He walked out, laughing and saying, "No doubt you are an excellent teacher, Radwa, because you were very convincing in your defense. Four of the members of the committee also voted to award you a distinction. One voted that it was a simple pass. Congratulations!"

The university whose halls, classrooms, and fields were filled with thousands of students only a month before now had only dozens. It was empty, still, and lonely.

I started working in an organized way to collect the material I would need when I was in Cairo. I would go to the library every morning, search for the books and periodicals I needed, take them to the photocopier, and make copies of the parts that were useful to me. When I went back to Prince House, usually in the late afternoon, I would eat dinner with my few friends who had not traveled.

One stifling hot day at the beginning of July, dozens of private cars and little buses started flocking to the university. Suddenly, the campus was filled with noise and movement. "What's happening?" we asked. We learned that the university administration had rented out one of the South West residence hall towers, some of the lecture halls, and the stadium to Guru Maharaji and his disciples. None of us had heard his name before and we started asking about the man and his story.

An American colleague told me that an Indian holy man, similar to the guru, had taught her a course in meditation last semester. "The guru taught us how to spend a few minutes without thinking about anything at all, he taught us how to control our power of stopping the flow of our thoughts completely."

Was I missing something or had I hit the mark in my judgment that my American colleague was young and stupid, and that her teacher was an ingenious fraud? I didn't articulate any of this but simply shrugged my shoulders and said, "I didn't come to university to learn how to stop myself from thinking!"

The face of the university changed on that July day when it clamored with thousands of young people who looked like hippies with their long, flowing hair, shabby, dingy clothes and bare feet. The university's cafés were filled with the scent of these many young people whose bodies hadn't been exposed to water in a long time. Groups of them were spread out around the lake and here and there on the grass, their body odor mixing with the smell of marijuana. The sight of them kissing was not confined to secluded corners or a boy and girl here and there. The university—administration and students—recognized same-sex relationships, and allowed gay students to have an organization to represent themselves and defend their rights; they had special dance parties from time to time in one of the coffee shops on the campus. Nonetheless, the sight of two men kissing each other in broad daylight at the university in the midst of all the comings and goings was not at all common.

For that first week of July 1974, the university transformed into a big hippie colony with all the trappings of the life they called the counterculture. Not everyone who came to the university to meet the guru had come from nearby—most of them had crossed the continent and come from the West Coast to this university in the northeast of the country, a road trip that took several days. Some of them came on a plane chartered for the occasion, which carried followers from Middle America and the South. That's what we heard, anyway.

Then we saw workers on the fields that sprawled out behind the South West towers, erecting a giant silk canopy surrounded by dozens of floodlights. "The guru will sit here, and from this elevated podium shaded by the silken canopy he will look out over his followers gathered below."

In the evening, those of us who were outside observers to this American scene headed for the fields. Before we got too near the place, the sound of loud, raucous music reached us. We wondered if there was a dance party nearby, and if the people attending it were unaware, or if it was purposely meant to spoil the Indian prophet's call.

We climbed to the highest hill near the student residence towers and looked out over the expanse of grass stretching in front of us. We saw the masses of humanity sitting on the grass—seven thousand, ten thousand, maybe more… Dance music was emanating loudly from giant speakers spread all over the place, and the followers of this eastern guru were responding to it by swaying while seated or dancing to its rhythms.

We forced our way through the crowd. The place looked like a doomsday scene, strewn with thousands of people, many of whom were disabled. We searched for a place to sit and found one near a young man who had set his two large crutches next to him. I heard someone call out to me and I turned. It was an Afro-American woman who I knew. Coming over to me she said, raising her voice so I could hear her through all the mystical hubbub around us, "The ship is sinking, what do you think?"

She let out a giggle that got lost in the general clamor and then left. I started thinking about lines from Eliot's poem "The Waste Land,"

> What branches grow
> Out of this stony rubbish? Son of man,
> You cannot say, or guess, for you know only
> A heap of broken images

What branches, I wonder, will grow out of this pathetic American scene? A sudden scream resounded through the air. People jumped up, some passed out—the guru had appeared.

On the podium under the spotlights stood a young Indian man of average height, with a round face and shining black hair half-covering his ears. It seemed clear that this Indian prophet was an adolescent boy who hadn't yet reached the age of seventeen.

Silence. The guru started speaking in the English particular to the people of India about love and the self that carries everything in existence inside of it, and in which people must search for the answers to all questions. The people were listening, hanging on to the face of this sincere young man who was repeating ancient Sufi sayings. I kicked my friend sitting next to me and said sarcastically, "All the questions about Watergate shouldn't be directed at Nixon and his administration, but rather at the self. Ask yourself my dear and you shall always find the answer!"

My friend laughed, and the scene went from being interesting to being boring so we stopped listening to the monotonous voice of the prophet. I thought about how much the poet Eliot predicted in his characterization of this malady and how perfect his choice was. The crippled civilization in the poem is today, a half-century later, crawling towards an old storehouse of inherited Eastern mysticism, relying on crutches to move forward. The poor guy sitting next to me who used wooden crutches to walk, did he come here hoping his devout leader would heal his amputated leg, which was probably lost in the Vietnam War? Or did he come seeking a crutch for himself, an image or some images to hang on the empty wall of his unhappy life?

Poor, deluded son of man…

We left the scene. We turned our backs on the thousands of people sitting on the grass and went back up to Prince House, still hearing the words of the Indian man through the speaker system.

"What a terrifying spectacle."

"They need a savior!"

"Not a savior, but salvation."

"And someone who won't hide behind trickery."

"There are always puppets of some kind who can present themselves in a savior's garb through their external appearance."

The next day, some films about the guru were screened and several so-called study groups were held, and in the square across from the main entrance to the campus they set up tables to sell cotton t-shirts with his picture on the front, cassette tapes of his speeches, and pins with bits of his hair stuck to them.

Jokingly, one of our friends said, "I was told that you could pay twenty-five dollars to kiss the guru's hand."

"I heard the same thing!" I laughed but I wasn't joking. I really had heard that.

In these last weeks of my stay in Amherst, the feeling that I was like a plant that had been deprived of water overwhelmed me. I was drying up. I started to dread looking at my face in the mirror. I combed my hair. I straightened up my body, fixing eyes on my hair and clothes; I feared meeting people's eyes and quickened my pace so I didn't glimpse that which followed me in silent reproach. I denied it and didn't deny it.

Despite this, leaving Amherst this time was different than the time before. I left behind places that I'd grown used to and friends who had given me a home in a place where I was a stranger. They went with me to the airport to bid me farewell. I embarked on my journey, kissed them goodbye, and went into the departure area. It weighed on me that I wouldn't see my Iranian friends again, because the two of them finished their studies and were preparing to go back home to their country. The flight from Bradley Airport in Hartford to New York City took half an hour; then I sat and waited for my jumbo jet to take off for Paris. After a nine-hour flight, I arrived in Paris—a city I had never visited before. I doubted that I could sleep in the morning in a new city, so I joined a bus tour that drove us around the city for a few hours. I dozed off while listening to what the guide was saying. In my sleepy haze I glimpsed the Eiffel Tower, and when the bus stopped so that the tourists could see the Notre Dame cathedral, I went to a nearby coffee shop and drank two cups of coffee before going into the church to look at its magnificent architecture.

I stayed in a simple hotel in a working-class neighborhood. I slept for two hours and then went back outside to look at things, but instead I listened. Was it my lurking nostalgia that made me hear something sounding like the *azaan* at sunset? But I did hear the muezzin's voice rising clearly in that poor working-class area. I followed the sound and before I reached it the azaan stopped, followed immediately by Farid Al-Atrash singing. I'd reached a Moroccan workers' bar that was the source of all these sounds. I stood at the door, one foot wanting to go in and sit down with whomever was there and the other aware that some of them might not understand what had come over this Arab woman who wanted to enter a space exclusively for men. I stood at the door, listening to the song until it ended, and then I turned back around with only my shadow as company, and we started walking through the new city hand in hand. I spent two days in Paris and on the morning of the third day I left for Cairo.

Chapter Eight

I locked the door to my room in Prince House and sat on the bed facing my two suitcases. One, I had brought with me from Cairo. The other, Anna had kept for me in Amherst. The strange, new room was lonely. The next day I would put a white cover on the bed and make the other bed into a sofa with a cover made of madras cotton fabric over it. In January there were no flowers I could put on the windowsill. I pulled back the gray curtain and saw the South West towers rising before me. The house director had assigned me a room without a roommate since I had become one of the house's old timers.

In the morning I woke up to the village I had left in the brilliant heat of summer and found that it was covered in white tree branches, heavy with snow. I took my blue winter coat and hat, my gloves, and my boots out of the suitcase I had left with Anna. Anna hadn't come back to live in Prince House, nor had my Puerto Rican friends. My two Iranian friends had left as well. I wondered who would live in the room next door—would my former roommate move in there? Her name was on the door with a colored sticker depicting a bride and groom. Had she gotten married, lost her mind, or both? After exchanging hellos and kisses in greeting, I learned that it was neither of the two. Doesn't someone write their name and profession on the door of their house to introduce who they are? That's why my colleague put her name on the room introducing her own deepest ambition—the dream of getting married!

I put the two chapters of my dissertation that I'd finished writing in Cairo on my desk. There they were: finally ready for me to show to my supervisor. These fifty typewritten pages were a source of anxiety for me on my journey—I worried about them and nothing else. When the airplane suddenly started experiencing turbulence in the heavy clouds surrounding New York before landing in Kennedy airport, I reassured myself that I had packed two copies of what I had written: one in my suitcase and the other in my hand luggage. But after circling above the airport, my papers and I finally arrived safe and sound. I organized them on the desk and then hung up two postcards I had bought at the Museum of Mankind in London on the corkboard hanging above it. One of them was a black-and-white picture of the small bronze bust of an African woman, made by an unnamed Yoruba sculptor. This is the most beautiful sculpture that I have ever seen. Of course, this tiny postcard couldn't do justice to it, but neither did it completely lose all sense of it. The other postcard was also glossy but this one was in color and depicted an embroidered Palestinian peasant dress. I put my clothes away in the drawers and then began contacting my friends to let them know that I had arrived.

My older Afro-American friend who came to Amherst in the fall as a visiting professor said, "Come over right away, I am waiting for you here! I am dying to hear all the news from Cairo."

I put down the receiver and braced myself to go out with my coat, hat, scarf, and gloves. I left Prince House to go to the town center where my friend was staying at the Lord Jeffery Inn. If it had been summertime I would have gone on foot, but in such bitter cold, I took the bus to town and crossed the street to Amherst College, which was right next to the small hotel that I was entering that day for the first time. The place seemed old and was primarily distinguished by what they call "Colonial" style. After asking at the reception desk, I started searching for my friend's room. The furniture and wooden walls of the building were shiny, despite being dark in color, as if part of a wealthy, white Southern family's house in the eighteenth century, I thought to myself. But this hotel was in a university town. If I looked out of the window now,

I would find no slaves working in vast cotton fields but rather male and female students who looked like hippies, perhaps reenacting the stories of the past.

My friend was staying in a room at the end of the corridor. I knocked on the door and she opened it. In the excitement of meeting again, I forgot the hotel and its architecture. My friend started asking me questions. She loved Cairo where she had been a political refugee following the coup against Nkrumah; she'd lived there for years in a house overlooking the Nile. Whenever I visited her she would say, "Sit down here so you can see this magnificent river!" Every time I nearly told her that I wouldn't mind sitting somewhere else. Seeing this view was like looking at my own face in the mirror. I nearly told her this every time, but I never actually did. When I sat across from the river, its presence surprised me, and I welcomed it as if seeing it for the first time.

"You left Cairo boiling—the workers in Helwan greeted the New Year with angry demonstrations in Tahrir Square, Qasr al-Nil Bridge, and Bab al-Louq, protesting against the deterioration of the economic situation. They arrested many of the people in the democratic factions, but the movement is ongoing. I ran into one of my acquaintances by chance two days before I left and he told me sarcastically, 'You haven't left yet? What are you waiting for? For them to arrest you first?'"

Shaking her head, she lamented, "My assumption was that this man would be an authentic extension of Abdel Nasser. He's half-Black as you know. I was encouraged by this."

What twisted logic is this, my old friend?

"Half-Black, or half-blue, color has nothing to do with it…"

Then my friend went on to gossip in the energetic way she and other older folks do… about what she was teaching in the fall semester, and what she would be teaching this semester, too. She spoke about her affection for everyone in the department. She talked nonstop, sentence after sentence, topic after topic. I listened to what she was saying while thinking about the telegram her husband W. E. B. Du Bois had sent to the First International Congress of Black Writers and Artists in Paris in 1956. At the time, Du Bois was almost ninety years old and had been persecuted by McCarthy in the years leading up to this, because when a number of people had renounced their relationship to Marxism and made public his membership in the American Communist Party, he was taken to court and had his American passport confiscated. In the telegram, he said,

> I am not present at your meeting today because the United States government will not grant me a passport for travel abroad. Any Negro-American who travels abroad today must either not discuss race conditions in the United States or say the sort of thing which our state Department wishes the world to believe. The government especially objects to me because I am a Socialist.

Then Du Bois warns Africa not to become a tool in the hands of colonial power, saying, "I trust the black writers of the world will understand this and will set themselves to lead Africa toward the light and not backward toward a new colonialism where hand in hand with Britain, France, and the United States, black capital enslaves black labor again."[3]

My dear friend and widow of the great activist—these issues have nothing to do with color! The activist's widow accompanied me out of the hotel and took the bus with me. She was youthful and active, like a woman in her twenties. She sat with me in one of the university coffee shops talking about Cairo and Amherst, her childhood, Nkrumah, Ben Bella, and Zhou Enlai. While I was listening to her talk, I was thinking about the hotel, named after the British leader Lord Jeffrey Amherst. The encyclopedia says he did very well in the British wars in the New World at the dawn of the eighteenth century. Two towns, one of them in the United States and the other in Canada, now bear his name. I wondered how well

3   *Présence africaine* 10, Nov 1956

Lord Jeffrey did in these British colonial wars? How many of the Indigenous inhabitants of the villages were annihilated? At what rate? Did his soldiers' guns mow them down or did he—as the lore has it—give them blankets infested with bacteria so when they got under them to sleep, they never woke up the following morning? The important thing is that the man did well in the war. There aren't any Native people left in Amherst… not even one.

The Lord Jeffrey Inn seemed small and nice and distinguished as I approached it to drop off my elderly friend, bidding her farewell at the door. As soon as she went in, I turned my back to it. But here I was in Amherst, which is located in the United States. I had just arrived yesterday, but I realized that I'd be here for the long months ahead. I decided to go back to Prince House to get the gift that I bought for Michael in London, and go to the department to surprise him.

I knocked on the door and went into his office. I pulled the string from the wrapping paper, saying, "It doesn't compare to the other picture that you have hanging in your house, where he is riding the horse in the forest. But this one is nice too!" It was a glossy picture of Guevara drawn in black ink on a bright red background. "This is so you have one to hang here in your office at the university."

I wondered if Michael's party would be big, like the one I went to at the end of last year in honor of his stepping down as the chair of the department. That night, the place had been crammed with guests and the corridors were overflowing into the kitchen, where people had started dancing. I thought the old wooden floorboards of the house would come crashing down under the dancers' feet as they pounded to the beat of the loud music. The resignation letter that Michael Thelwell had presented to the president of the university, and we had all read, revealed that this tall, young Jamaican man who had not even reached thirty years of age when he founded the department of Afro-American studies—to which he really devoted himself in the years that followed—was a distinguished and talented man who was different from other people. He was like a chivalrous knight riding through the American forest. I went to this party in his honor at the house of one of the other teachers in the department. It lasted until the dawn hours when the guests left as a courtesy. When morning broke, everyone left as if in tacit agreement and silence prevailed. Then a Black woman from the South began intoning slave spirituals, people's songs from the fields. Her voice rose, cutting sharply into the tranquility of the night, as if allowing for creation to witness the pain of time, face to face.

Why are Afro-American gatherings characterized by such vibrancy, as if people are carrying baskets in which to collect the fruits of the endurance, joy, and sorrow that they reaped over the harvest of a lifetime? I went to another Afro-American party, a wedding, when Michael married his girlfriend Casey, the mother of two beautiful children. I went early, carrying with me my wedding gift of a shawl that I had bought in one of the little corners of the ancient Cairo souq where the little alleys branch out from the central square and the Al-Hussein mosque, with its one graceful minaret. This sunshine-colored Egyptian peasant shawl was a gift that suited Casey's glowing bronzed skin tone. I went into the house that was once again crowded with dozens of guests. Michael was wearing a flowing African shirt with black lines in geometrical patterns. There were few white guests—the bride's mother and some professors who were Michael's friends. Why in exile do we clutch onto our roots like this and attend every gathering affirming our identities? Is it fear or nostalgia? Or is it a pride in our tales of adversity? When I saw my Ghanaian friend wearing a white African shirt, decorated with Arab embroidery around the collar, I realized that my dress too was sewn with silver needlework. Unlike how they dressed every day at the university, all of the Africans had come wearing clothes particular to their regions or countries.

Since Michael was a foreigner in the United States and a newcomer, none of his family attended his wedding. He stood greeting the guests and welcoming them, playing the roles of both the groom and his family. He had prepared the wedding food himself, a huge quantity of Jamaican dishes like rice and peas, mixed and spiced with hot peppers.

The tiny, sixty-something wife of a professor with her silver hair in a bun said to me, "Radwa, my father was a Jew from middle Europe, but not at all a Zionist." Did I notice an apologetic tone in what she had said or was I imagining it? Her words surprised me. I knew that her husband, my PhD supervisor, was of Jewish origin, but I also knew that he was a communist. I wasn't expecting the issue of religion to be raised, at least not just like that with no reason. The woman had drunk that certain amount that makes a good person long to be better to others, and closer to them in order to communicate and break down barriers, exposing their anxiety about being accepted. This woman appeared to be about my mother's age. I wanted to kiss her and say kind words to her, but I hadn't drunk enough to overcome my own shyness.

The corridor where I was standing with the professor's wife contained the only source of light in the living room of the house, whose lights were mostly low. The room had turned into a crowded dance floor. A young Afro-American man was blowing a little metallic whistle from time to time, in the background and at breaks in the music, in a way that was extraordinarily lively and fun. A light-skinned, bearded Black man with a smiling face was speaking in a loud voice, elongating his words with the particular rhythm of Black American speech. Michael—the groom—was coming and going, like the mother of the bride in Egyptian folktales. One of our nasty departmental colleagues sidled over to me, like an old gossiping yenta, and whispered in my ears, with his eyes glistening, "Do you know what's happening outside?"

"What?"

"A woman drove here from Washington, and she's standing outside the house saying that if Michael is going to get married, she is first in line, and she threatened to throw stones at the house. She must be crazy!"

Laughing, I responded to him, "If we stay here in this lovely country for too long, who knows how things will end for us?"

My elderly Afro-American friend responded, "Do you know that Michael chose to get married on W. E. B. Du Bois's birthday?"

When I passed by him, my professor leaned over and shouted in my ear so I could hear him over the raucous music, "I read your two dissertation chapters."

He moved his mouth away from my ear. I was staring at him inquiringly, waiting for more. Then he leaned over again, "In your chapter on the Harlem Renaissance you focus on the writings of Alain LeRoy Locke as if he was the only one... We'll talk about this in more detail, in any case. We'll talk about it another time."

If only I had been able to withdraw into a corner and sort out the anxiety that my professor's words filled me with. But there was nowhere to sit. My eyes scanned the room, looking for somewhere to stand quietly for a few minutes. The young man with the whistle was asking me to dance. I followed him, saying, "I'm going to disappoint you. I'm not a good dancer and this kind of dancing is going to expose how bad I am."

The young man laughed, saying, "I'll teach you!"

Why do lighthearted people make you feel comfortable and relaxed? I didn't know this young man, but he taught me the dance and reminded me of my three dear siblings. Minutes before, when I had danced with a white man who taught in the English Department, I was surprised that he didn't look at me while he was dancing. Why did he ask me to dance then? He was totally self-absorbed and didn't look at the person right in front of him. This man reminded me of the characters in "The Waste Land" who walk in a circle, their eyes fixed on their feet. "I have heard the key / turn in the door once and turn once only." Eyes turn away and withdraw, locking the gates of the soul and confirming the isolation of the prisoners, despite the whole world. Why did this white American man ask me to dance? It depressed me! This Black American man taught me the dance and I wasn't embarrassed by the weight of my body faltering in the movements. And he called me sister in the way Afro-Americans refer to each other. He danced and blew his whistle and laughed and chatted. He had brought a special gift to this wedding celebration, the gift of joy!

I proceeded with writing the third chapter of my dissertation at the same time that I was revising some sections of the two chapters I'd already written in Cairo. My professor's comment on the night of the party had made me anxious. The very first thing I did when I woke up the next morning was read what I had written with a careful, critical eye. When I met with my supervisory committee a few days later, I was surprised that they praised my work. It seems that my professor's comment was from what he'd read previously. I left this meeting having been given a push that propelled me to the library, where I worked hard to improve what I'd written and finish the remaining chapters that had started to take on a final shape in my mind.

I started working diligently and consistently. This was no longer just because I wanted to finish quickly but because I had been taken hold by a genuine interest in the subject I was researching, once again.

Often I spent the morning in the library stacks, finishing one section or another that I felt was incomplete in my dissertation. In the evening and at night I sat in my room, which had become the place where I could be alone to put my thoughts together, organize them, and write.

On a long day, I would leave the library at noon to have a quick lunch at the café in the center of the campus facing the library building, then go back to the library or my room to finish working. At the beginning of each month I would get the newsletter that contained all of the cultural programs offered by the five colleges and choose the events and exhibitions I wanted to attend.

Nothing could stop the enthusiasm of the small woman wrapped up in a heavy coat who covered her head with a woolen shawl to go down to Hampshire College to watch a Chilean film. The bus was late and the bite of the cold stopped a person from thinking of anything else. The snow was overwhelming and the temperature was twenty degrees below zero. This woman was like a little hedgehog wanting to hide from everything. But she isn't a hedgehog. The bus was late, her nose frozen. On her return it was even colder but what she had watched was unparalleled, and then next day she would go watch another.

When there was a lot of empty time, eating dinner alone was depressing—the woman found her food lost its taste. *Hey, Anna, tomorrow do you want to come and eat dinner with me? Hello, Suzy and Clara, can you come next week and eat with me? What do you think, Rashna, about coming with Rajinder to have dinner with me? Yes, or now if you want.* The taste of the food is different when you are with friends and can substitute their companionship for the feeling of foreignness, of eating while staring out into an empty room with only a shadow for company, with the spontaneous bustle of food preparation. This desk that she had covered with white paper turned into a smart dining table. She arranged paper cups and plates on it and then everyone sat down to eat, chat, and smoke while waiting for the water to boil to make coffee at the end of the evening.

But friends don't come every day. And the food is the same evening after evening: a piece of chicken, wrapped in tin foil, and cooked quickly for a half an hour in the oven, a can of boiled corn and another of beets poured over it. I would put this all on a paper plate and it would become a quick dinner to prepare and eat. Then I would drink a cup of coffee and go downstairs for the most exciting event of each day that would break my routine—the seven o'clock evening news in the Prince House television room. I would sit in front of the big television perched on its raised shelf and follow the latest world and local news, interrupted by commercials for novelty products: toothpaste, washing powder, nutritious foods for cats and dogs, underwear, bank loans. Then the presenter would follow with the news. When the broadcast ended, the dozen or so people who were in the room watching would go their own ways. We'd all go back to our work. I would return to my room to write drafts of chapters in English that I would add to the parts of my thesis I'd already completed. And then I would write letters in Arabic overflowing with a lonely woman's longing for Cairo.

Chapter Nine

The snow melted and it seemed that spring was coming even though the trees remained the same, fierce winds blowing through their bare branches. I carried on with my studies. I was still managing to persevere and achieve despite having differences with my housemates. I used to wait daily in front of my small mailbox for a delivery that would bring either joy or nothingness. Sometimes I would get a newsy phone call in the evening from my older Afro-American friend who followed events in Egypt on her big black radio. March sunk deeply into me and then ended. April arrived with its heavy rains and I was in terrible pain from rheumatism. Is this the cruel April of Eliot's poem, when a lonely body's pains are turned round and round by rainy desire? Or is a body's longing for April's fertile earth so intense it can be painful? From the window of my room, I would watch the rain pouring down endlessly, unabatedly, and then go back to writing.

My new housemate next door introduced herself and invited me in for a cup of coffee. She told me excitedly about her work as a volunteer in the Peace Corps in Thailand. When you speak about your noble mission to spread civilization to the tropical forests of Asia, you ignorant, evil American woman, your coffee sticks in my throat. I began to feel frustrated by the frequent trips abroad of another American woman from the Faculty of Education who I'd met when I first arrived at Amherst. When we ate together, I would always think, "Do those clear hazel eyes carry only goodness within them, or do I just not understand anything at all?" But everyone on campus knew about the relationship between the Faculty of Education and the US Agency for International Development. She regularly traveled to Iran to participate in a literacy program there, and I would ask myself: "Is she evil and I simply don't understand human beings, or is she stupid and simply being used?" This country doesn't make us safe. I made myself small and carefully retreated into a shell I had created in order to protect myself from the people working within the system.

I attended a lecture by a leader from a community of Indigenous people. He was speaking about the American Indian Movement established in 1968, and the more than twenty organizations united within it. I listened to his talk about the government's frequent violations of the agreements made with Indigenous Peoples. "We have made three hundred seventy-one treaty agreements. All were made only to be broken. The Indian lands that the US government should not interfere with were indicated within each treaty, and each one was violated so that now the ghetto is the only place left for us." With a smile on his face, this thin man said, "I have thirteen children... This is also a kind of resistance!" There was a distinguished looking man sitting in front of me wearing a color-ful beaded necklace and a zigzag-patterned sweater, with his hair done in two braids with a leather headband around his forehead. He brought a real place out of a fake, cinematic context and gave it a place within history. I learned from it and became a part of it.

I burst into enthusiastic applause for the Chilean men on the stage wearing traditional capes and holding Andean flutes. Were they mourning their dead, glorifying life, or doing both things at the same time? They discussed the massacres there. I listened to Allende, the widow of the primary target of the coup, narrate it in some detail in a small church near Yale University in New Haven. Some friends of mine and I then went on to attend a one-day conference about CIA activities. One cold April evening, we stood waiting for the church door to open so we could hear Mrs. Allende's lecture. I cheered along with the crowd for a govern-ment of national unity and "*el pueblo unido jamás sera vencido* / the people united will never be defeated." I cheered as if I were one of the Chilean people being chased on the streets with nightsticks and tear gas bombs.

The massacre was mentioned repeatedly. I bought two records by Victor Jara and my Puerto Rican friend Anna translated the words I couldn't understand. One of the records had his famous poem on the cover about the 5,000 prisoners in Santiago Stadium. Jara wrote it before they cut off his hands and killed him. Are these massacres haunting me? Or do they haunt this era and I am simply a spectator?

I passed by a store downtown that sold snacks and drinks. I went in and stopped to the right of the doorway, where I noticed a small card with a drawing of a camel on it among a dozen other cards. I stopped and stood in front of this little camel like a child who has just seen herself in the mirror by accident. What made me pause there? Was it the unusual drawing itself that made the camel look like a cartoon from a children's movie? Or was it the sad, disappointed look in the creature's eyes? I paid the saleswoman with coins and took the card. As I was walking to the university, I recalled lines from Ahmad Dahbour's poem "The Palestinian Boy," about a child who survived the Black September massacre.

> Deliver us, Camel of Burdens, for our path is made of thorns
> And it is only by using your molars that they can be torn

When I got back to my room, I sat down, took out the little card and wrote a few words to Mourid about everything.

I was at peace with myself and the world in the last days of April. However, not long before this, there was an incident during dinner one night when I could have strangled my neighbor, the former Peace Corps volunteer. We were in my room and she said that Egypt crossing into the Sinai in 1973 was an attack that amounted to an invasion. It took a huge effort on my part to explain everything calmly.

I had not been in such a calm and peaceful state since I arrived in the United States. Was it the feeling of relief after wearing heavy winter clothes and finally being able to see the green trees through the windows? Was it my feeling of achievement for only having the introduction and conclusion of my dissertation left to write? Was it Mourid's new poem "Said the Villager and the Sweet Water of the Spring" that I received by mail as a pleasant surprise and for which I sent congratulations by telegram? Or was it everything all together, and something else I found in newspapers, news bulletins, and people's faces? I was waiting for Mourid to arrive in mid-May. I wanted to surprise him by telling him that I had submitted the entire dissertation to be typed up before showing it to my supervisor, and that as a little gift I had translated his long epic poem into English.

Therefore, I started working like I was on a construction site. I was writing the dissertation, translating the poem, and participating daily in National Liberation Movement Week. We were working to oppose Zionism, distribute our literature, and declare our solidarity with representatives of democratic, nationalist Palestinian organizations. I would watch the television news to find out what was happening in the Vietnam War. And at nightfall, the construction site would calm down and Radwa would close her eyes to sleep till the next morning came.

I sat on a bench on the sidewalk, waiting for the bus and thinking about the thin, young Indigenous woman who played the traditional flute during Liberation Movement Week. Why did her words disturb me? Was it because listening to these stories up close is disturbing? Does history pull us along like a waterfall? Is all hope lost? Your stories scare me and your flute pains me, but what can we do? I took a yellow bus bearing the name of the university to New York, carrying a videotape of a movie that I needed to return. I went to the post office downtown, gave the person behind the counter the tape and waited for him to tell me how much it cost to send. I was thinking what good luck it was that we had chosen this film. It was a documentary titled *Revolution until Victory*, directed by a group of young Americans. Through multiple documentary photographs, it compares Nazi crimes against Jews to Zionist crimes against Palestinians. The response exceeded our expectations, so we screened the film three times, and every time, the audience would sing along with the *fedayeen* at the end of the movie with rousing applause and repeating the word *"fedayee"* in the song. I wish Mourid had been here, so he could have seen the film and come with me that night to the concert by a Dominican band.

Before returning to Prince House, I passed by a diner and had a quick meal of a hamburger and a cup of coffee, and then went home. I washed my face and sat at my desk to finish some work before going to the party at eight PM.

The band Expresión Joven was performing on April 29 in one of the rooms in South West Hall to commemorate the tenth anniversary of the US invasion of the Dominican Republic. The concert was on the last night of Liberation Week, which had been organized by many nationalist, democratic organizations at the university.

The room was crowded with students who had participated in Liberation Week activities over the previous six days. Although the hall wasn't big and there was no stage, everything was prepared to host the band. A small wooden platform was set up with rows of chairs in front of it, leaving standing room on the side for those without seats. When the band entered the room, it felt like a huge crowd was surrounding the four musicians. One of them opened the concert with a political speech. Then the band started with a song by Victor Jara followed by an original song. One of the band members started teaching the audience the chorus and asked them to sing along. For the last six days, emotions had been running high and they ran even higher at the concert. Everyone sang along. A girl whose face was pale sat next to me. "I thought I was coming to a concert, not a protest," she fussed. I smiled and replied in a loud voice, so she wouldn't miss a word, "Well, I knew!" and continued signing along

93

Was our excitement that night a result of the success of the week we had organized? Or was it because the band and their songs were so good? Or was it that in watching the news every day we'd started to realize that this era was ending in our favor, even though we weren't expecting it to? And what more festive and joyful atmosphere to announce this news in? An omen arrived. He didn't descend from Mount Olympus, nor did his features resemble poetry or mythology. He was just a slender guy with shoulder-length blond hair dressed in a worn, thick woolen shirt and a pair of dark blue jeans. He walked up onto the stage where the band was standing. They stopped playing as he approached the singer holding the microphone and whispered in his ear. Then the singer shouted, "Saigon has fallen to the revolutionaries!"

Watching the scenes of the last macho Yankees evacuating Saigon through the roofs of their embassy into waiting helicopters caused mass public hysteria. The American flag had fallen among the ruins of the Vietnam War. The system had to deny that scene by showing others that would satisfy both its nationalistic pride and also its illusions about itself. Thus, the media started glorifying America the beautiful and its noble, heroic dream. It depicted America as a loving imperial mother, even if some of her children were ungrateful for all she'd given them. Television stations began airing interviews with American families who had adopted Vietnamese children years before.

Media outlets began reporting on American transport planes that were bringing hundreds of Vietnamese children to the United States to save them from the horror that was afflicting their country. Americans sat in front of their televisions watching President Ford on the seven o'clock news welcome these children at the airport, holding one of the babies in his arms. No doubt, many men and women who believed in that American deception they call a dream secretly or openly shed a tear watching this scene designed to tug at the heartstrings and affirm American beneficence. No doubt also, there were many people aware of the nightmarish nature of this dream who lived their lives outside of its context, and who followed this scene with a mix of relief and bitterness because they knew it so well. Perhaps they mockingly laughed at this "transcendent nationalism," cursed the system and its lackeys, or had a drink while remembering their anti-war protests to toast the newly liberated city, and then went out into the world carrying the transgressions of Vietnam as one more heavy burden on their backs, like so many of the nation's previous crimes.

But as for us coming from the rest of the world, the brothers and sisters whipped by the stinging lash of imperialism's whip, the news of this liberation and the raising of the revolutionary flag in Saigon was not merely the joyful media story we had been hoping for. It was also something that we related to, something at the very heart of our own stories, histories, and futures. It affirmed that, at the end of the day, what we believe in, what we say, what we expect, and what we are planning, even if it doesn't seem so, is what is right.

Imperialism's flag had fallen and we saw how it was done!

Chapter Ten

We each took one side, my roommate and I, and together we started unscrewing the fixtures on the two beds. We then lifted the metal frames and put them next to each other under the room's large glass window. We put the mattresses back on top of them and then covered them with a big white sheet as if they were one bed. Then we put the blue blanket decorated with little white flowers I'd bought the day before on top of it. When we were finished the room had transformed from one that had two single beds on bedframes, one of which I had used for sleeping and the other as a sofa, to one with a double bed raised only a few centimeters above the floor. I was finally ready to welcome Mourid.

I had finished writing my dissertation only two days before. I had delivered a complete draft to the person would type it out before presenting it to my supervisor. After searching I had found a suitable apartment in a good location and had made an agreement with its owner, who was also a student, about when she would vacate it. Then I spoke to Mrs. Robinson, the director of Prince House, about Mourid coming and informed her that he would stay with me in my room for the four days until we were able to move to the apartment I had rented.

On that sunny day in May, everything was how I wanted it to be. I cleaned the room in the morning, prepared food, took a shower, got dressed, and put on my makeup to get ready to go to the airport. I wore a skirt and sweater—my woolen skirt was two-toned, light gray and dark olive green, and my long-sleeved fine woolen top was open necked and also olive-colored. I wore a silver necklace with a beautiful, antique silver Kabyle pendant from Algeria that rested against my chest. I put kohl around my eyes then brushed my unruly shoulder-length hair. One last look in the mirror and I was shocked and surprised at how beautiful the woman looking back at me was. What had happened to this little woman when she prepared to meet her love, what happened to her that made her shine like a star, or a poem? When such joy inhabits Radwa does it suit her, like the scent of lilacs wafting through the open window at twilight? Or is it the feminine that suits her? I put on my shoes and stockings, and then called the airport to be sure that the airplane was on time.

How many times, Mourid, have we been separated, and how many times will we meet again? How many times will I experience that heartbreak that lodges in the throat during time passed alone inside the customs area, sitting and ignoring that weight in the pit of my stomach while waiting for the announcement that the plane has arrived? Why is it that whenever we are separated or meet up again, I picture you in perfect detail: your walk, the turn of your head, your short hair, the way your small eyes look behind your eyeglasses, your eyelashes, even the shape of your shoes and the color of your socks?

Through the glass window of the airport waiting room I spot you coming, and a gentle joy flutters over me, like the moist green head of a baby bird, cracking through its white shell and emerging. You come out to me and we are together in person. We hug—like a girl and boy whose minds are lost in passion and happiness, running like two colts. But there is no place for horses to run in this modern American airport whose buildings look like wooden matchbooks. We each experience this reckless and wild feeling of joy inside ourselves, as we sit next to each other in the car that will take us from the airport to Amherst, together this time.

In my university room, we shared news and kisses. We ate dinner and then sat on the bed, drank our coffee, smoked and experienced that beautiful atmosphere between two old, close, intimate friends who have met up again—the mood of sharing, chatting, and coming together after being away.

Mourid brought me Arabic coffee, the Cleopatra cigarettes I liked, and details about what had happened in El Mahalla El Kubra. He told me, "The workers staged a sit-in. They went on strike and controlled nearly the entire city. I heard that they demonstrated in one of the squares, hanging whatever meat and chicken they could find on a rope and then on the other side facing it they hung balls of falafel. Then the central security forces broke into the city after they had besieged it for days, and occupied it."

"Did they open fire?

"Yes, and a number of workers were killed."

"How many?"

"I don't know, but at least ten is what I heard."

Did we unintentionally slow our pace when walking into the village, or was our pace already slow because we didn't have to be at any particular place at a particular time? Perhaps the movement of our bodies and legs were not slow but heavy. "They kill us because they are afraid," I started repeating to myself and then told Mourid.

"They are terrified," Mourid replied, "Even Umm Kulthum's death represented a real burden which they don't know how to deal with. They fear the masses of people taking to the streets— even if it is for a funeral procession."

"Can you believe that for several days they kept publishing conflicting stories in their newspapers about Umm Kulthum's health? One day she was 'clinically dead,' then the next day she was 'still with us.' It's like they simply feared the sudden emotion of the people, or simply the people feeling anything, even sadness! When Umm Kulthum died, they broadcast her more emotional songs over and over, completely ignoring all of her songs linked to the nationalist sentiments of the fifties and sixties."

I had watched the end of the funeral on a televised news broadcast. The sea of humanity swelling around her coffin didn't surprise me as it did the American students who watched this scene with me. They started asking me earnestly about the story of this singer whose death evoked such great sadness in so many people. I replied to them that this woman was very famous, much beloved, and had reigned over the music scene in Egypt and the entire Arab world for more than twenty years. Perhaps my answer convinced my American colleagues, perhaps not. But when the news was over and I went back up to my room, I knew that what I'd said didn't explain the unique way in which this woman touched the people. Was it her human presence, powerful intelligence, and her talented voice, which opened the way for "Ms. Umm Kulthum Ibrahim" to transform from being a young woman singing religious folk songs about the life of the prophet Muhammad in a tiny village in the Nile Delta, to become the Arab diva who synchronized radio dials all the way from the Gulf to the Mediterranean Sea, as people tuned into her Thursday evening concerts at the beginning of every month? Was it her talent itself or that this talented woman represented a more general desire, which she embodied and whose rhythm was able to unite people at this moment in history? Was she herself one of the features of this historical moment? Can this woman be dissociated from Nasserite sentiment and the Arabs' joy and pride in discovering that they were a nation united? Is anything more fitting than this woman's songs to embody the distinctive duplicity of the Arab bourgeoisie in its aspirations for independence, while leading the national liberation movement and its recidivism into the past? Is the emotionality of the Egyptians normal, or is it a distinguishing characteristic of this people? Do we feel more love and more sadness, or do we simply express what others don't express?

I didn't especially love Umm Kulthum or care to attend her concerts; in fact, her sentimental songs and their outdated, Ottoman-style relationships between men and women offended me. Expressions like "*uzul*" for "separation," "*shajn*" for "sorrow," "*jawa*" for "tender," or others that spoke of "turning the embers in the fire," or "my oppressor" and that made up the lexicon of her songs, were in my view far from a healthy context for relationships between the sexes. But truth be told, I responded to the woman when she stood as a nationalist institution raising her unrivaled voice to pronounce, "Egypt should speak for itself" or "Truly it is the time for arms." Her vibrato would shake up any woman who was living what she was singing. I responded as if her voice were water, and I a parched, thirsty plant.

"But Mourid, did they even broadcast 'Egypt is in my blood and soul?'"

"Not even 'Egypt is in my blood and soul.'"

"So they decided to deny her authentic nationalist side and instead emphasize her other side. They are completely coordinated among themselves, in their perverted decision to do this."

On the days that followed, we went together through the town streets and the trees on the hill, following them wherever they took us, running through wide open grassy lawns, meandering around the hills, dragging ourselves up the mountain path, wild lilac bushes surprising us. We sat in their shade, chatting nonstop. We took the yellow university bus or the town's public bus wherever they would carry us, getting off at nearby villages and the other colleges in the area, going into coffee shops that were new to us, sipping their coffee, eating their fast food and then continuing happily through the streets with our tiny instant camera. We'd stop passersby, "Could you please take our picture?" The person would do it politely and unwillingly, and like two stupid kids we would stare at the camera in his hand, laughing at his cold, scornful look, and he would think we were smiling for the camera.

We collected our belongings, bid farewell to Prince House and everyone there, and moved to our new place in the center of the town. It was a small two-room apartment at the top of a stone three-story house. Like two birds that built their nest on a church steeple, Mourid and I lived under this house's pointed wooden ceiling that sloped down on two sides at the kitchen and washroom. You couldn't stand up straight but had to bow your head for fear of banging it. Mourid made fun of me, saying, "So tell me how many times did your head hit the ceiling today?" I alternated between wanting to laugh and feeling the pain in my head where I'd banged it. From the big window next to the bed, we could see the grassy lawn around the elegant little church whose one bell had a clear ring, which we heard while sleeping sometimes, as if it were part of a hazy dream. Then Mourid's glasses frame broke and we hurried to the nearest place that sold glasses in town. "Sorry," the heavy-set woman in the shop said, handing the glasses back to me, "I don't have the right frames." We had to go to another shop, and we were able to relax when the stylish blond man standing behind the wooden counter told us that it would be possible to exchange the broken frames for another pair. We sat and waited on the soft leather chairs next to the displays of round frames until the young man's sputtering voice reached us. "I am very sorry, but I cracked one of the lenses."

He held out his hand with the new glasses frame with the cracked lens in it, "I'll make a phone call right now and order a lens to replace the one I broke. They'll send it to me by post you will have it in four days!"

We paid for the new frame and left with the broken glasses. Mourid was irate and I followed him silently. We met one of my colleagues from Prince House, who commented to Mourid, laughing, "It's a great way to see America for the first time, through broken glasses!" Four days later we went back to the young man who greeted us with a victorious smile, handing Mourid the new glasses. We exchanged smiles and words of thanks and left.

"Now we can go to New York as we had planned," I said turning to Mourid. "Problem solved, and it's nice warm weather, too." I stopped to look closely at his glasses. The new lens had darkened in the light of the sun, but the other one had remained clear as usual!

Mourid took off his glasses and looked at them, then shot off back to the shop like an arrow, with me scurrying behind him. The young man said in a calm, brassy voice, "I broke one of the lenses, that's all I am responsible for!"

"But if you had told me that there was a possibility that the glass would be different, I would have ordered two new lenses! How could you have possibly thought that anyone could wear glasses like this?" Mourid spoke sharply and energetically.

The young man started dialing his phone and replied in an exaggerated manner. "I made a mistake in trying to help you change your frames. I shouldn't have even touched those poor-quality frames with lenses that we no longer use in the United States! Come back in four more days."

When we finally got the glasses back with matching lenses and turned to leave the shop, the young man was talking to himself in a low voice. When Mourid pushed the door open he raised it a tiny bit, saying, "If you set foot in this shop again, I'll break your legs!"

"What is this idiot saying?" Mourid asked me as we were walking outside. I answered him sarcastically, "He said that our glasses, the way we look, and perhaps even ourselves are of inferior quality and don't deserve to be in his fancy shop!"

"Is what he's saying true?"

I pulled him by the arm, laughing as I said, "Now let's go see America!"

Chapter Eleven

We stood under an umbrella in the cold, gray, rainy weather, waiting for the bus to take us to New York. It came and we got on. Four hours later, we reached the city. When we got off, we asked for directions to the hotel where we were staying, and then realized that we could walk there. We walked down a big empty street looking for 34th and Broadway, Mourid carrying our small leather suitcase. Though it was raining, I'd closed my umbrella because of the fierce wind. I felt like it was my first time visiting the city even though it wasn't.

"Do you remember the short story by Ahmad Hashem al-Sharif about a young clerk from the countryside who was carrying a bag when he came to Cairo for the first time? His fear—or rather terror—of losing his bag represented his fear of getting lost in the big city." I laughed. "Watch out for the bag!"

He feigned a serious tone. "Watch out for the umbrella."

We crossed to the other side of the street that was suddenly filled with people and stores, both small and large. After walking a bit, we noticed a hotel. When we asked, it turned out to be the one we were looking for, that had one floor reserved for students with rooms at a lower rate. We went to the office for student tourists on the twentieth floor and I showed my university ID. "That will be $20 with no breakfast," they said. We paid, took the keys, and went to the room.

As I closed the door, I smiled and said, "We made it to the hotel without losing the umbrella!"

Inside, a list of instructions printed in small letters was hanging on the door:

1. Don't leave the door to your room open when you're inside. Lock it with the deadbolt.

2. When you leave the room, turn the key twice to ensure the door is locked.

3. Take care that no one is watching when you leave your key at reception.

4. Do not open the door to anyone unless informed by the receptionist that you have a guest.

5. The administration is not responsible for any items left in your room. Leave all money and valuables in the hotel safe.

6. For your own safety, if anyone threatens you and asks you for your money, hand it over to them immediately.

We looked at each other and laughed, but when he went to the bathroom, I locked the door. After we showered and changed our clothes, Mourid locked the door with the deadbolt, turning the key twice when we left.

We took the elevator to the ground floor and left our passports in the hotel safe. Then we went off to eat and have a walk through the city streets. We ate fast food—burgers and fries—and then had a coffee. Afterward, we went back out to see the Empire State Building, which was only a few blocks away. While waiting for the green light to cross the street, I said to Mourid:

"Even though I've been here three times, I've never visited this building. On my first visit, I went to three museums all in one day like a crazy woman. The second time, I was too busy with the stories of a Lebanese friend of mine about the boyfriend she left behind in Beirut and the never-ending ups and downs of their relationship to see the city. On my third visit, I met some of the city's most important leftists. I was staying with my older Afro-American friend at a house belonging to a friend of hers. The two of us went to a little "family gathering" in her honor.

Everyone there except me was in their sixties. They were all of that generation who had lived through McCarthyism in the 1950s."

Standing in the seemingly endless ticket line to enter the Empire State Building, I said, "That's a long story. I'll have to tell you all about it later."

We took the elevator up to the lookout point. It was not yet five PM, but it was so cloudy it seemed like dusk. When we went outside, a fierce wind blew right in our faces, whistling through our hair and over our bodies. New York lay right there below us, for miles on end. Fog obscured its details but we could still see the skyscrapers scattered in clumps like mushrooms.

"I can't see the Statue of Liberty," Mourid said.

I tried to find the statue and took my city map out of my purse to figure out where it was. My eyes scanned the city searching for it. I pointing out into the nothingness: "I think it's over there."

"It probably disappeared in the fog."

I started searching the map again, and pointed at a group of tall buildings: "That's Wall Street, the center of business and capital."

The wind was whistling in our ears and sweeping against us as if trying to make us lose our balance. As we walked to the inner balcony to warm up in an enclosed area, I told Mourid, "This high up, skyscrapers don't seem as tall as they do when you are standing below them. In Boston, there's a group of tall, thin skyscrapers that look like they might collapse at any moment. Whenever I stare up at their balcony-less facades, black glass hiding the people inside, I feel scared... terrified even."

"Perhaps we should come back again on a sunny day so we can see more than fog and cement. Do you want to get a cup of coffee?"

We pushed open the glass door leading out to the busy street. We held hands reciting verses from "The Waste Land" by T. S.

Eliot. Mourid would say a line and I would follow up with another.
Then I would say a line modifying the poem, with my own words:

> Unreal city under the brown fog of a winter dawn.
> I had not thought death had undone so many.
> Unreal city under the gray fog of a summer dusk.
> Vienna, Paris, London, unreal!

Mourid put his arm around me and we walked in the streets, enjoying the crowds and streetlights, observing the city that we both
knew and didn't know.

We got dressed and went downstairs looking for a diner where
we could have breakfast. We went out onto the street that seemed
empty of people compared to the night before. I looked at my
watch; it was not yet eight o'clock in the morning, on Saturday.
It was cloudy, but not as cold as the day before. We went into a
little diner on the next street over and sat down on raised chairs
at the wooden counter. Mourid asked for a fried egg and coffee
and I asked for toast with cheese and a piece of cake with my
coffee. There weren't any other customers in the diner except us
and an old man who was sitting at the table behind us, silently
eating his breakfast. Then an older woman wearing a coat came in
and sat down at one of the tables near the man's table. Her eyes
darted between the server—whom she was waiting for to bring
her food—and us.

"Older people feel the cold more. That poor woman is wearing
a coat in the middle of June!"

"Strange that she went out for breakfast in a diner so early in
the morning." The woman had started talking to the man across
the empty table between them.

"Maybe she lives by herself and is lonely."

The server put the breakfast we'd ordered down in front of us
and we started eating in silence. I thought about the old man in
the Hemingway story who went every night to the same café and
sat there until it was closing time and all the other customers had

left. I remembered a dialogue in the story between two waiters about how he tried to kill himself. "Why?" "Nothing!" "Nothing?" "Nothing!" This expression was repeated in the story like the tolling of a bell, reflecting the lonely, crushing nothingness that the man knew so well. He refused to leave the café, "A Clean, Well-Lighted Place." It calmed the fear inside him. I lifted my eyes from my cup of coffee. The man walked out, leftover food still on the table, while the woman sat hunched over staring out into nothingness. Her open coat revealed what she was wearing underneath. She still had on her nightgown, but she hid the hem by hitching it up with a belt she'd fastened around her waist.

"Should we go to the Statue of Liberty… or should we go to Harlem?"

We paid for our breakfast and went out onto the street without having decided where we were going. We walked back in the direction of our hotel but then we passed it and crossed 34th Street. We went to Fifth Avenue, walking by the fancy shops that give the city and streets their identities. On Fifth Avenue, I recited Langston Hughes' famous poem about Harlem to Mourid—the one that begins with the well-known line "What happens to a dream deferred?"

This poem is intense and stark. It evokes Harlem's realities and the details I have been living through my studies. A train spits out smoke and races through the city, looking out over the North Atlantic and a woman holding aloft the torch of freedom. People fleeing cities in the South wanted freedom to find freedom here. Black and poor, they came to the city holding their children in one hand and in the other suitcases filled with clothes, memories of the past, and a dream. But *York al-jadida* doesn't like the mixing of races. Doesn't this woman's face reflect Europe? New York chooses its deep-seated whiteness and leaves Harlem to the Blacks. It became the capital of their poor, their professionals, their artists, and their soldiers who returned from the First World War with ideas about the people's liberation. The twenties saw the streets crowded with Black people enthusiastic about the marches of Marcus Garvey. He wore his trademark clothes and embroidered hat while calling for Black Nationalism and the return to Africa. Newspapers and magazines talked about Civil Rights and National Liberation. Poems sang out: Black is Beautiful. Soft piano music filtered out of nightclubs, as did angry saxophones and the voices of rebellious preachers. Orators standing on street corners talked to the people about Socialism, revolution, and the fundamentals of the struggle.

Years passed Harlem by and imprinted on it the identity of poor people and their ancient race. This big ghetto became the capital of the oppressed, born hating the police and the rich and needing to smash things up. They smash themselves and each other up with bitterness and spite. They smash up their oppressors with collective explosions in the face of the white power structure, represented by its resources and its police force's repressive powers. "Radwa, do you see that group of people gathered over there? Come on!" Mourid dragged me by the hand to cross the street toward a group of men with shaved heads wearing loose white trousers, their chests covered by a thin piece of light orange fabric similar to people performing the hajj. Some of them were beating drums. "So these are Hare Krishnas, then?"

"They're calling for peace and love."

"Cool!"

"Do you see how these young people seem spiritual, and live as ascetics, far away from the world and its struggles?"

"We were talking about Harlem. I bet they can't go near it. Something might happen to them, or at the very least the Harlemites would mock them."

I said, laughing, "You're such a poet! You're always flying up in the clouds above us, do you have wings?"

We weren't far from the Metropolitan Museum of Art, and, although I knew Mourid is usually not that enthusiastic about museums, I asked him if he wanted to go in. I tried to encourage him, telling him it had a large Egyptian collection as well as other rare collections, including one of Greek art. "I've been there before. How about we go in?"

Mourid replied, "How about we spend the day in the streets? Come on, which is better? Seeing hundreds of irrelevant paintings and sculptures under dull neon lights, moving from one hall to the other with the smell of shiny wooden floor varnish surrounding us? Or getting to know the city better by spending time in its streets?"

So we spent the entire day on Fifth Avenue staring into shop windows and people's faces, commenting on what we saw and how much things cost, joking and laughing, agreeing and arguing, chatting and saying nothing, and then chatting again. We went into a bookshop to ask for a book, left having bought only that one book, and then crossed the street to Washington Square in Greenwich Village. Our feet ached from the long distances we'd walked, and we felt extremely hungry.

"Mourid, aren't you sick of hamburgers?"

"When I'm hungry, all I care about is eating."

"When you stay in New York for a long time, you'll surely come to hate hamburgers. The first week I was here, the university cafeteria hadn't opened yet, so I used to have lunch and dinner at the university's Blue Wall Café every day: plain hamburger, cheeseburger, hamburger with eggs, deluxe burger."

"Until hamburgers ran through your veins!"

"And I was afraid of getting food poisoning!"

"This is a pizzeria. You like pizza."

We opened the door and went in; the heat of the place seared through us. It was small. Against the wall there was a thin wooden bar and a bunch of high wooden stools for people to sit on. There was another bar facing it. Behind the counter stood a brown-skinned man with a bushy moustache, black hair, and dark eyes. His shirt was sticking to his chest with sweat. The man was working fast, like a machine. He kneaded the dough and put ground beef, mushrooms, tomatoes, and cheese on top of it. Then he slid the pizza into the oven behind him. While waiting for our turn, I whispered to Mourid, "That guy is Arab or Iranian."

"How do you know?"

"From the way he looks."

"Maybe he's Italian."

"No, he's wearing a gold necklace with the Ayat al-Kursi from the Qur'an on it."

"Maybe he's Turkish." After ordering our two slices of pizza, I asked the man:

"Are you Arab?"

He looked at me with a smile on his face: "Yes. I'm Palestinian, from Jerusalem. And you?

"I'm Egyptian, and this is my husband, he's Palestinian."

"*Ahlein, Ahlein!*" The man said and then stopped working. The atmosphere shifted. A big smile lent his round face, rosy from the heat of the oven, an air of kindness and youthful excitement.

"Do you two study here? I've been working here for a few months. I was here last November when Abu Ammar came and gave a speech at the United Nations on behalf of Palestine. It was something to celebrate—I even cried."

The young man started making our pizza. There was no one working, except him and one other person behind the counter. There were many customers standing in line behind us, waiting their turn. The guy couldn't speak to us more, so he expressed his warm wishes through the pizza he was making. I started watching him as he took two balls of dough, rolled them out, and added extra meat, tomatoes, and cheese—more than usual. I looked at Mourid, whose eyes were fixed on this man's hands as he was making the pies. He remained silent as we ate the pizza. Once we were finished, the man said enthusiastically: "Come back again!"

I thanked him, and Mourid gestured his goodbye, saying, "Take care of yourself brother, take care!"

We had been walking for a long time when we finally reached

Washington Square Park, so we sat on a bench next to a group of people who looked like hippies. One was playing the guitar, another the panpipes. We sat calmly smoking and listening to them play. We watched the pigeons that gathered in a particular spot of grass from which they would suddenly fly away, leaving behind just one that walked slowly and moved its neck in that strange way that pigeons do.

"Who's going to bring us a cup of coffee?"

We left our spot and walked toward the street. In this park, there were a number of spots of green grass where pigeons alighted, followed by the eyes of old men and women sitting on wooden benches. On one of the benches, drunken people sat apart. Their wrinkled faces on tired heads nodded against their chests, so still that they appeared to be asleep. One of them was staring into space, having a conversation with the air, himself, and any person who approached. He had a paper bag next to him, in which he hid a can of beer or bottle of booze. He would stop talking only to take a sip. Young hippies gathered around here and there, playing music, smoking, and telling jokes. We spotted a group of people that included many children and as we got closer, we saw that the children and adults were all laughing.

When we squeezed ourselves through the crowd to watch, we saw that people had made space for a skinny young man with shaved blond hair and a black shirt, pants, and shoes. He was a mime. He was trying to open an imaginary glass window. He bent his back slightly, lowered his shoulders, drew in a breath, and using his strong arms, pushed the imaginary glass up. He started bending backwards more and more, his facial muscles tensing as he lifted the air with all his strength. He pushed and pushed, and then jumped backwards so that the imaginary glass wouldn't fall and crush his thin fingers. People applauded him, and he bowed with a smile before repeating the scene once again.

Steps away at the entrance to the park stood a brown-skinned man from the West Indies. He was wearing brightly colored,

African-print clothes and standing in front of two big barrels, explaining his art to the passersby.

"They say that these old metal barrels are garbage cans, and we answer that they should be for the people's enjoyment. Brothers and sisters, look! These two metal barrels are a simple musical instrument. They look like garbage cans, but they can do great things... Listen to this!"

The man started hitting parts of the barrels with his stick, making different sounds each time. "I'm just showing you first, but now I'll play some real music for you." The round-faced Black man with the sparkling eyes started beating the barrel quickly and powerfully, making his rhythmic and irregular beats into a beautiful melody. His body swayed back and forth to the sound, as if he himself were a third drum joining the other two. His perspiring face made him all the more powerful and charming.

"And our coffee?" Mourid said finally.

"Let's take a bus to the hotel and have coffee somewhere closer to there."

The sun was setting and it was almost dusk, so we wanted to drink our coffee, eat something, and get back to our hotel room before dark. Two strangers in a city that they both know and don't know.

"What's happening tonight?" I wondered out loud, because of what sounded like hundreds of police sirens racing back and forth through downtown.

"Maybe this happens every night, but we didn't notice it yesterday because we went to sleep early," Mourid said.

There was no balcony so we couldn't see what was going on, but there was a small square window right at the top of the wall through which the lights of the skyscrapers entered the room. But we couldn't see the neon greenish-blue lights of the police cars as they patrolled, sirens wailing.

We sat in front of the television, Mourid lying back in bed and me on the chair across from it. We were both looking at the screen but not following what was going on. We would start chatting about something and then we would stop. It seemed that we were still preoccupied with what was going on around us. Our door was locked with the deadbolt and key, and the security instructions were hanging there. We were aware of this, and also aware that we were in a twentieth-floor hotel room in Manhattan. We listened to the sounds of the street like prisoners who were connected to the outside world only through the sirens.

"Let's guess what's happening now!"

"They found a dead body."

"Or there was a bar fight!"

"Or a car was stolen!"

"But that happens everywhere."

"Let's guess more…"

"A rich woman discovered her diamond necklace was stolen."

"There was a museum robbery."

"Or a bank!"

"Or a house!"

"That happens everywhere, too!"

We got really into the game.

"Some guys broke into a store and smashed everything up!"

"A poor Puerto Rican woman killed herself."

"Neighbors reported a bad smell coming from the house of the elderly man next door whom no one had seen for days!"

"The cops shot a Black man!"

"A girl was raped and beaten to death!"

"Ten guys got drunk and committed mass suicide!'

"This is a depressing game. I'm going to take shower."

"Shall we go to the Statue of Liberty?"

"Let's go to *Guernica*."

We pushed open the door of the hotel that led out onto the street and walked down Thirty-Fourth street to Fifth Avenue, and then we crossed and turned left so we could go to the Museum of

Modern Art. "It is starting to rain!" I looked up and saw gray clouds were covering the sky. Mourid opened his umbrella and held it in his left hand. I walked beside him, holding on to his right arm with both of mine, and talking nonstop about my previous visit to the museum.

At the door, we shook out the umbrella to get the water off of it, folded it up and went inside. I turned to Mourid and whispered, "Before we go upstairs to see *Guernica*, I want to show you a little secret." We went into the exhibition hall. A small painting the size of a school notebook was hanging next to a number of other small paintings, in its usual place on the wall. "I wanted you to see this painting!"

We stood there and looked at Picasso's *Minotaur* that he created for the cover of *Minotaure* magazine in 1933. I felt the same way that I had on two previous occasions. I felt that the look in the legendary bull's eyes was speaking to me meekly and innocently, with sadness or defeat, and also perhaps to other kinds of creatures and spaces whose emotions escaped me, though I was paying close attention.

"This poor Minotaur of the legend is carrying the whole world on its shoulders!"

"I feel for it, like it's me."

"Why did you say it was a secret?"

"I don't know!"

We went up to see *Guernica*. We walked into the room through the main door. It covered an entire wall: a painting the color of newspaper photographs… black, white, and gray. At the top right corner, a person is raising his head and hands calling for help through a square of light, but failing. Next to him, a woman, whose head is plunging out of a window, is resolutely holding onto a small, lit kerosene lantern, which is touching a bigger lamp that looks like a cross between a light bulb, the sun, and an eye. And at the bottom right of the painting, a woman is running right into the middle of what is happening, terrified, and straining her neck looking up—fear has distorted her fingers, toes, and nipples. In the center, a whinnying horse is swooping down with its legs broken. The dead horseman underneath it is fully dismembered. His head and hands are separated from his body. His eyes and his mouth are wide open, wanting to scream, or perhaps ask, "Why?" One of his palms is open, and its distorted stiffness recalls both the man reaching for the window and the running woman carrying her murdered son. This horseman is holding a flower and a broken dagger in his other hand. At the top left of the painting, there's a bird straining toward the light. Was it slaughtered? The prominent head of the bull is a serene witness, permanent like the soil of the homeland or the natural cycle of life.

"Maybe I called that little painting a secret because I was thinking of it in the shadow of *Guernica*."

"You like the Minotaur, but *Guernica* is his real statement. It's his commentary on the massacre."

Then we went to look at a collection of sketches that Picasso had begun a few days after he learned about the bombing of the village. On April 27, 1937, Nazi warplanes bombed the village of Guernica in Basque country to assist Franco's fascist forces. The bombing lasted three hours and resulted in the death of 654 people, with 884 injured. In May, Picasso drew six sketches related to the event and then more only days later. On May 10, he started painting. It was finished in June. The painting was then moved from Paris to New York where it was exhibited at the Museum of Modern Art, until it was taken to the Prado in Madrid in October 1981.

"Picasso had the image of the distressed woman leaning out of the window with her lantern in his mind right from the beginning—it was there in the very first sketch," I said.

"And the horse, too."

"Indeed, some artistic statements are magical, as the Prophet said."

"Anger is not the only reason for an artist's magical statement. An artist must also have a powerful ability to use geometric rigor to produce something that is significant, simple, and harmonious."

The rain was falling heavily onto the glass roof of the gallery and was increasingly loud, imposing itself on the place and on us. I told Mourid that there were other paintings by Picasso in the museum, a nice collection by Modigliani, a painting by Siqueiros that we shouldn't miss, and another painting called *Zapatistas* by a Latin American painter whose name I forgot. But I was expecting that right after seeing Guernica he wouldn't want to look at anything else, as was the case with me the first time I saw it.

"Why don't we have a coffee?"

We went down the stairs to the first floor, looking in the museum's directory for the café. We went through a glass door that led to a garden holding a few statues. It was still raining heavily and the garden was empty. We found an arrow pointing towards the café. We walked through the door. The café was small, warm, and elegant. We sat and started eating silently.

"What are you thinking about?"

"About our massacres that no one has painted yet!"

Sitting across from Mourid, I was sipping my coffee, smoking, and thinking that *Guernica* is the most famous political painting of this century. I was pondering what makes art Art, what makes it different, what distinguishes it from everything else. Then I looked down at my coffee cup and was disappointed to find it now empty.

"Should we have another coffee?"

I got two more cups of coffee with steam rising from them and we sipped them calmly before continuing our tour. When we opened the glass door leading out into the garden, it had stopped raining.

"Shall we go out?"

Steam was rising in the garden. The damp grass and leaves were heavy with crystalline raindrops. We stepped into the garden as if we were newly arrived people on brand new land. Bronze statues gleamed with moisture. There was a large statue of Balzac by Rodin, a wrought-iron goat by Picasso, and another sculpture called *The Family* by Henry Moore, which was the figure of a naked woman lying down above a little stream of water surrounded by greenery. The weather was so cloudy it felt like twilight and the statues made their presence known in the absolute silence, which enveloped the garden. This made a tiny bit of fear seep into me. Were these statues frozen or were they like the ones that Emir Mousa of the *One Thousand and One Nights* saw in the City of Brass, where life was frozen for a fleeting moment?

Did this place—haunted by statues, green, and rain—frighten me? Or was there something in this place that felt unique and intense like the moment of conception, which overwhelmed my spirit, causing a tear to fall from my eye?

"Mourid, what makes art, Art?"

I didn't wait for a response, but took his hand. We turned our backs to the garden, pushed the glass door open, and walked back inside the building.

After hours looking around the museum, we went back out, carrying our umbrellas and walking down the street that was no longer wet. The streets were packed with pedestrians coming and going, as well as cars and buses, as if we'd just returned from a trip and our eyes had to adjust to a different light. We went back to commenting sarcastically on the museum's contemporary art wing, the last one we'd visited in the museum. In one corner there was sawdust and an old tire from a car, as a work of art. A wooden toilet seat with a window around it was another. Mourid laughed, saying, "I guess we've become conservatives!" Then he opened his umbrella against the rain that had started falling once again.

We paid the hotel bill, picked up our small suitcase and umbrellas, and walked out onto the street. There was enough time for us to go and watch the Puerto Rican Day Parade. After that we'd go to the main bus station, eat lunch in a nearby diner, and get on the three PM bus back to Amherst. We walked to the corner of Thirty-Fourth Street and Fifth Avenue and turned left, heading toward the neighborhood where the parade would take place.

Before we had even arrived, we heard the sound of drums. As we got closer and closer, the beating of the drum was accompanied by the distinctive noise of a crowd gathered for a popular celebration. We started to make our way through the thousands of families crowded on the sidewalks and tried to find a foothold we could see from. It was clear that the normal traffic had been diverted for the cars and floats participating in the parade. They started to pass in front of us, covered in brightly colored, shiny materials, with raised flags and giant banners with the names of Puerto Rican community organizations on them. Atop the floats were dark-skinned Latina beauties, wearing open-necked short-sleeved dresses, tight around the waist and flaring wide around their legs, or wearing open gowns that left their arms and legs exposed, with colorful scarves. Then groups of children, young men, and women marched by in tight, well-organized rows, followed by rows of workers, and groups representing every kind of activity common in the Puerto Rican community.

We were amazed at how huge this parade was and even more amazed by the numbers of people crowded onto the sidewalks. Thousands of men, women, and children, tens of thousands, so many that their vibrant human fabric completely covered the street's asphalt: brown faces, multi-colored clothes, red, blue, green, and purple balloons. The hands of the young and old were holding thousands of little flags made of paper with a blue triangle and red and white lines, stuck on small wooden sticks. People selling ice cream and hotdogs had set up wooden tables, patriotic young guys had stickers on their shirts and trousers saying, "Proud to be Puerto Rican" or "Kiss me, I'm Puerto Rican," and curvy young women wore metal earrings decorated with the Puerto Rican flag. The Puerto Rico that lived in New York came out onto the street to help dissipate some of its fears by looking at itself in the mirror, collectively, in all its distinctiveness.

A thin young man approached us and offered to sell us one of the radical newspapers. Smiling, I told him, "I can't read Spanish."

He walked away from us angrily, thinking that we were lying to him, because he didn't believe that we weren't Puerto Rican. I shouted after him, "*Compañero*, we're Arabs!" I don't know if he heard me, and he was soon lost in the crowd.

"The American eagle pounced on their island, taking it as prey in 1898, and is still eating away at it today. I can't believe that there's such a huge number of Puerto Ricans in New York!" Mourid observed.

"A third of the island's inhabitants emigrated to the United States and they primarily work in New York and Chicago." I replied. "But in the States, they face various problems linked to poverty, unemployment, not knowing the language, and not being able to adjust socially and culturally. They are living at the bottom of the race-class ladder, which of course increases their nationalist feelings as Puerto Ricans. Despite this, a friend of mine told me a while ago that if they held a referendum today about either becoming independent from the United States or finally joining it as a new state, there is a large possibility that the result of the referendum would be to join... Can you believe it? It's clear that the economic and political policies of the United States toward the island have made Puerto Ricans feel that being deprived of US citizenship—the thing that allows them to migrate here looking for work—puts them in a quandary. They feel so disgraced that they have to think twice whether or not it is better for them to take refuge in Imperialism. The radical groups and organized political parties are sensitizing folks to the seriousness of such a position. Imperialism is merely the wings of the eagle swooping down to pounce on them!"

"We should head to the station now so that we don't miss our bus," Mourid prompted.

I replied jokingly, "Did you really come to New York and leave without visiting the Statue of Liberty, or should we buy a little statue and send your friends a postcard with a picture of it?"

"Let's ask that family for a Puerto Rican flag!"

Chapter Twelve

When I went to hear my professor's opinion about my dissertation, he teased me by saying, "Why don't you write a thesis with the mastery with which you translated Mourid's poem, 'Said the Villager' for me?"

"So you liked the poem, then?"

"I really liked it, it's Whitman-esque."

His wife laughed and said, "For him, no one will ever match Whitman!"

"Do I understand from this that you didn't like my dissertation?"

He laughed. "I didn't say that."

The professor was sitting on a sofa beneath a window that flooded the room with light, as had recently become his habit. He had next to him a little table, with stacks of books and papers on it, and also the metal walking frame that he'd started using to move around since he'd broken his leg the month before. I sat next to him so that I could listen to his detailed comments on my research. When we finished, he said with a smile, "Now we can set the date for your dissertation defense. What do you think of June thirtieth? If that works for you and for the two other examiners, I'll inform the university officially. Then, my dear, you'll be the only one to ever have had your examination on this beautiful balcony overlooking the forest, here in this house."

According to my supervisor, his proposed changes would not take a huge amount of work, only an hour or two that I could do between now and then in the library, looking up some specific references, or at home, reworking imprecise paragraphs and unclear sentences. But when I had finished the research and the subject I had been working on through these years started to lose some of its appeal, I was again plagued by questions. I was like a carpenter who takes his new work to show people, and asks questions about all kinds of things that have nothing to do with wood, nails, glue, or anything related to carpentry.

We were still living in the very same house whose wooden floorboards creaked whenever we went up and down the stairs and in which we had to be constantly vigilant not to bang our heads against the sloping ceiling in the kitchen and washroom. Mourid and I were happy to be together and experience these little details of our shared life with one another. We did everything together—went to do our daily shopping, carried our dirty clothes to the laundromat, cleaned the house, cooked food, browsed in shop windows, went to cafés, sat on the grass, and looked out the big window of the bedroom at the heavy rain pouring down on the asphalt, the lights of cars, and the streetlamps. We would always go out into the street to smell the damp grass when the rain stopped. We were delighted by the charm of a Black musician, playing his loud brass horn like a new prophet. Michael would bring his two stepchildren over or invite us to his house where his wife's son once surprised us by trapping a snake. My elderly friend would unexpectedly drop by the department barefooted and wearing shorts, to invite our Afro-American friends and us to her house. We would go around to their houses and mix in their circles as if we were a part of them.

While waiting for the defense, I would characterize our daily life as having a pleasant routineness that made some of the things that were strange and unusual seem routine and familiar.

"We got a package!" Mourid said, opening the door and bringing in a little cardboard box with postage stamps all over it. Like two curious children craning their necks, each impatient to see the surprise first, we pulled off the string and opened the box.

"Mangoes! And flowers!"

Anna had sent us four different kinds of mangos and gardenias from Puerto Rico. In a Cuban film she and I had seen months before, a young man had asked a young woman, "What's your name?" She answered, "Louisa." He replied, "No, it's Gardenia!"

"What's a gardenia?" I had asked Anna at the time. She had explained it to me and now she was sending one—a white flower with a pungent scent, which she'd wrapped in a moist cloth so it would reach us still in bloom. The blossom still had not totally wilted yet.

My Indian friend, Rashna, had called me on the phone and proposed that we accompany her and her friend Rajinder on a road trip to Canada for five days. I was excited about the idea, but Mourid was worried.

"And the defense?"

"It's on the thirtieth of June—we will be back four or five days before!"

We took Rajinder's old Volkswagen that sunny morning, heading north to the border with Ontario, Canada. Rajinder sat behind the steering wheel, looking elegant as always, his head wrapped in a turban that his Sikh religion required. He also wore a silver bracelet around his wrist. Rashna sat next to him looking from time to time at the map she'd brought that would show us the way. Mourid and I sat in the back seat. At noon, we stopped to eat some of the sandwiches we'd brought with us. The car broke down and we went into a village along the way to fix it. The sun was setting and we hadn't yet reached Toronto. Then night fell. We stopped on the outskirts of the city to eat again and Rashna called a friend of hers who'd invited her to stay at her place. We'd drop Rashna off first and then look for a hotel. But we were lost in the big city. We asked for directions, continued on, and then lost the way again on the mountain rail tracks in the endlessly pouring rain. We finally arrived after one in the morning.

The woman whose house it was invited all of us to stay the night with her. "It's very late for you all, and we're far from the city center. Rashna will spend the night here with me in the house. There's a little shed in the garden with space for the three of you." A little wooden shed in the rain in the forest... it was an image from a poem, but despite this scene, I was exhausted and I couldn't sleep. Was it the strange place or my fear of the thunder and sounds of the rain beating down on the roof of the shed, which made it feel as if it might collapse? But in the morning after a night of rain, the garden shone like a lover who woke after a night of romance. This forest after the rain was fantastic, heavy with moist green, thick, ancient tree roots shining as if they weren't old at all; their ancient mud whispered enigmatic things about fertility and the seeds of creation. We walked around this place waiting for our friend to finish wrapping his turban and combing his mustache, rounding the two sides upward a bit according to Sikh tradition. We drank our morning coffee with the woman who owned the house and thanked her. Then we confirmed our reservation for the coming three nights at the hotel.

We looked around the city. We visited the art museum, the science center, and the provincial parliament. We also browsed in the shopping areas. We were shocked and astonished looking in the windows of the many sex shops, like country folk. We went down back streets where ethnic communities of Indian, Chinese, and African origin dominated. We met some of Rajinder's Sikh acquaintances who had taken off their turbans and silver bracelets, and shaved their beards and moustaches to fit in better, though they still remained outsiders. We finished our visit by staying one night at Ontario Place, which featured various kinds of clubs. In the morning, we left the city like good tourists who'd had a good time but whose knowledge of the place was fleeting and superficial.

On the way home, we stopped to look at Niagara Falls and spent a few hours there. We went down inside the earth in an elevator to enter the wide-open canyon. We traded in our shoes for rubber boots and wore coats with hoods to protect us from the water. Then we entered the tunnel that would lead us to a balcony where we would see the waterfalls surge above our heads. The tunnel was filled with the roar of rushing water like the sound of rotating lathes, ovens, and machines in a huge factory. The sound was deafening and we had to scream to hear each other. The water made our faces wet and we laughed like children, alternating between fear and the joy of adventure.

We went up to walk alongside the stone walls that lined the river, and looked at the rush of the waterfalls. Mourid took a photograph of me. In it, I appear sitting on the wall with the falls behind me, in my blue clothes and my hair pushed back behind my ear with a thin black band. Even my small brown shoes swinging above the ground appear in the picture, but you couldn't see either the burning feeling within me, or anything of the site itself!

Then we went back to the old Volkswagen that we'd gotten used to—like the lonely traveler is used to his donkey—and headed south. Darkness fell on this little box that held the four of us as we took to the road. Rajinder and Mourid took turns driving and Rashna and I shared memories in the backseat, whispering in low voices. Rashna spoke about her father and mother, both of whom had passed away, as well as the traditions of her Zoroastrian religion. She talked about her father's sister who wouldn't forgive anyone for smoking a cigarette in her presence because it disparaged sacred fire. She spoke about her brother who had a child and named him Riyad. "Isn't that an Arabic name?" We stopped twice to fix the car when it stalled, and once to eat a quick dinner. The chubby woman working at the diner laughed and asked us, "Should I put onions on your hamburgers?" Then she carried on, her laughter mixed with a slight tone of complaint, "I love onions and my husband doesn't. I only eat them when I travel!" We said goodbye to this woman and went back to our German-made chariot, which this time carried us to Amherst without fail, and we arrived two hours past midnight.

I turned on the television and sat on the ground, leaning my back against the wall to watch a program about police investigations.

One episode of it ended and another began with the title, "Beware of Child Trafficking!" The announcer said, "There are many families who are not able to have children, and they deal with this by adopting. We have a case like this here today, with its own particular circumstances."

The woman, Ms. M from the state of Virginia, found herself pregnant and didn't want to have the baby and bear the responsibility of raising a child, especially since she wasn't married. After she gave birth, a rich family from New York who wanted a white child of Jewish origin offered to adopt her child. Since Ms. M met these specifications, she signed an agreement with a lawyer as follows:

The adoptive parents will take on all the expenses of Ms. M during the time of her pregnancy and delivery.

The mother will hand the child over directly after the birth.

After this she will be paid a specific sum of money that they agree upon.

"Mourid, come here."

The announcer moved to an interview with the woman in her house in Virginia. She couldn't have been more than twenty-five years old. She didn't seem particularly intelligent or gifted, nor did she seem stupid. He asked her, "Why didn't you want the child? Because you weren't married?"

"Not exactly. I wasn't ready for the responsibility of having a child. My lifestyle doesn't really allow for a child."

"What happened? When you signed this agreement, I mean?"

"They took me somewhere in Florida, where there were other young women in my same situation. We were pregnant and did not want children; we'd decided to give our babies up for adoption."

"For a fee?"

"Yes, to pay the cost of care during pregnancy and delivery."

"Then what happened?"

Mourid came, carrying a tray with a pot of coffee and two cups. I told him, "Sit down quickly. This woman sold her baby when she was still pregnant!"

"I moved to New York to give birth in a hospital there," the woman replied to the TV interviewer. "A day after giving birth, according to the contract I had signed, I had to hand my baby over."

"Did you see the baby?"

"No. They wouldn't let me. I had to hand him over immediately. So they covered him and gave him to the adoptive parents with the lawyer present. Now, a year later…"

"Don't you feel anxious or worried? Don't you miss the baby?"

"Not particularly. I didn't see him and wasn't connected to him."

"So what happened one year later?"

"The lawyer called me and told me that the adoptive family had discovered that the child's responses weren't normal, that he might be different and they didn't want him. I don't know, of course, if any of this is true, but the contract didn't cover this kind of situation."

"This means that you still don't want the child?"

"As I told you, I don't have room for a child in my life. Also, I have never even seen this child. Maybe it's not even my son. Then there is the contract…"

Getting up to stand near the window, Mourid said, "It's the one and only American Dream!"

But I didn't say anything. I stayed in place, glued to the television screen, but stopped watching the episodes of the program that followed. I was thinking about the solution in Thebes of Greek mythology—Oedipus killing his father and sleeping with his mother without knowing. Then the plague spread through Thebes and infertility afflicted his family. This woman signed a binding legal contract agreeing to hand over her son, trading his rights for money spent. What curse would befall them? Oedipus had his eyes gouged out. And this well-dressed blonde woman was blind and unfeeling.

While getting up to go to the bathroom, I said, "It's a truly American ending!"

My professor said, smiling, "Now give me the paper." This was the indication that the exam was finished. I handed him the printed piece of paper that had the title of my dissertation, my name and the names of the three members of my examination committee, along the words, "I approve of the form and content." He signed the paper and passed it to the other members. While he put his hands on the table in front of him to help himself stand up, he said, "Now come over here!"

Then, with a paternalistic mix of authority and affection, he said, "You're a good girl, you did excellent work!"

He kissed me and the others kissed me and congratulated me. But my professor saying "You're a good girl" had given the moment a familiarity that was different from the typical way such an academic achievement would be awarded. This simplistic expression was just like him, just like students always publicly called him Sid, the nickname for Sidney, or like the tennis matches he played with his students, or the casual tennis shoes he always wore.

As I started to organize my papers in order to leave, the weather outside was sunny and warm, and the sounds of singing birds filled the air. Laughingly, I told Michael, "Now you can drive your car as fast as you like. But it would really be sad now if I died in a car accident when I was on my way back from my dissertation defense!"

We left my professor's house the same way as we came—Michael in the driver's seat, Mourid in the seat next to him, and me in a semi-comfortable position right on Mourid's knees. In less than twenty minutes, we were at the Amherst hills, but Michael passed them and we entered a neighboring area. "Where to?"

"Somewhere really magnificent!"

He started driving on a narrow, curving mountain road that the rays of the sun almost couldn't reach because of how thick the trees were. Tall trees that seemed to have no tops, surrounded by small trees and plants that were only several inches high, trees that had soft, tall trunks and others whose trunks were wrinkled and which appeared to be split open, even from far away. There were trees with large leaves the size of two hands stuck together and others that had tiny leaves. The green of the trees and the brown of their trunks were interwoven, their colors mixing. The three of us pondered the scene in silence. I broke it by saying, "I wish I knew the names of all of these trees." Michael said, "Jamaica is even greener than here!"

Then we were silent once again and I felt exhausted. Did I look the same as in that picture at Cairo University, after the announcement of the results of the scholarship competition for master's students? I had taken off my traditional black university gown that I'd worn to the examination, and I stood with my friends and colleagues so they could take a picture of us. My broad smile—especially for the picture—was exhausted, and this was clear on my face. We left the Faculty of Humanities to meet the Cairo night, its fall weather and pleasant hubbub. The university clock was striking eleven PM. Was it the ritual nature of this scene? Or was it the familiarity of friends and everyone coming together to share it? Was it this woman feeling content because she'd achieved her old dream of belonging somewhere? Or was it all of these overflowing into a beautiful moment for a happy occasion?

Michael was still pressing on through the mountain roads, but not so quickly this time, with me sitting on Mourid's knees. Our eyes met and he patted my shoulder and whispered, "Congratulations!"

I smiled at him and remembered that even when I was about to finish my secondary school degree, my father was still alternating between refusing to let me enroll at the university and being enthusiastic about wanting me to pursue higher education. I said, laughing, "One year before I went to university, my father said that anyone who let their daughter study at university was stupid!"

Michael said with mock seriousness, "I agree with your father about that."

We all laughed, and it seemed as though our laughter drew a kind of line between the silence we had gotten so used to, as we were looking at the green of the hills, and our loud conversations that followed.

After Michael took us home and left, Mourid said, "Wait here, I will go up and get the camera ready. I want to take a picture of you!" When he came back, camera in hand, I told him laughingly, "A commemorative picture!"

"It's on the occasion of you earning your advanced degree!"

"My grandmother Fatima, my father's mother, would never pray for the advanced degree. But in her prayers she used to say, 'My dear Radwa, granddaughter, may God bless you with a perfect groom and a house full of life!'"

I stood in front of Mourid, who started taking a few pictures of me. A month earlier I'd turned twenty-nine. Not bad, I said to myself, thinking of the sarcastic words of my math teacher who taught me at lycée, "All I ask of you all is to have one ambition. I will have succeeded if you all receive your middle-school diplomas and take them with you to your marital homes and tell yourselves contentedly, 'I am an educated woman.'"

I smiled at the camera and the idea that I, who was afraid of the words of my teacher and a life of seclusion that awaited me, had once again succeeded in jumping over a hurdle, and escaping. In the pictures that we got back the following week, there was a petite woman, quite thin, with shoulder-length black hair, wearing a brown shirt and short skirt, not hiding the smile dancing on her lips. Her face was pallid and bore traces of exhaustion. Were these the final traces of the examination, or the exhaustion which follows a huge leap that forces the person jumping to summon all of her strength?

Chapter Thirteen

"It is the Fourth of July, American Independence Day!"

"The beginning of next year's bicentennial celebration of the Declaration of Independence."

We passed by many shop windows decorated with American flags. We bought newspapers and sat on a wooden bench in the park near Amherst College to read them. It was summery weather and getting hot.

Mesmerized by the eloquence and bravery of what I was reading, I said, "Listen, Mourid. This is the speech of the Afro-American leader Frederick Douglass who was born a slave, educated himself, and bought his own freedom, becoming an advocate for the liberation of slaves in the middle of the nineteenth century. The *New York Times* has reprinted some excerpts. This is a speech he gave in Rochester, New York, on July 5, 1852, titled, 'What, to the American Slave, is Your Fourth of July?' In the introduction, Douglass asks his audience, which is white, of course, 'Why am I called upon to speak here today? What have I, or those I represent, to do with your national independence?'

"After this introduction, he says, 'But, such is not the state of the case. I say it with a sad sense of the disparity between us. I am not included within the pale of this glorious anniversary! Your high independence only reveals the immeasurable distance between us. The blessings in which you, this day, rejoice, are not enjoyed in common.

"'The rich inheritance of justice, liberty, prosperity and independence, bequeathed by your fathers, is shared by you, not by me.

The sunlight that brought life and healing to you, has brought stripes and death to me. This Fourth of July is *yours*, not *mine*. *You* may rejoice, *I* must mourn. To drag a man in fetters into the grand illuminated temple of liberty, and call upon him to join you in joyous anthems, were inhuman mockery and sacrilegious irony.'

"He then carries on, 'My subject, then fellow-citizens, is AMERICAN SLAVERY. I shall see, this day, and its popular characteristics, from the slave's point of view. Standing, there, identified with the American bondman, making his wrongs mine, I do not hesitate to declare, with all my soul, that the character and conduct of this nation never looked blacker to me than on this Fourth of July! Whether we turn to the declarations of the past, or to the professions of the present, the conduct of the nation seems equally hideous and revolting. America is false to the past, false to the present, and solemnly binds herself to be false to the future.'"

"Let's keep this issue of the *New York Times*; this speech is an important document. Perhaps we'll find the complete version in the library and we can copy it so we can save it. Carry on!" Mourid implored me.

I continued, "'Is it not astonishing that, while we are ploughing, planting, and reaping, using all kinds of mechanical tools, erecting houses, constructing bridges, building ships, working in metals of brass, iron, copper, silver and gold; that, while we are reading, writing and cyphering, acting as clerks, merchants and secretaries, having among us lawyers, doctors, ministers, poets, authors, editors, orators and teachers; that, while we are engaged in all manner of enterprises common to other men, digging gold in California, capturing the whale in the Pacific, feeding sheep and cattle on the hill-side, living, moving, acting, thinking, planning, living in families as husbands, wives and children, and, above all, confessing and worshipping the Christian's God, and looking hopefully for life and immortality beyond the grave, we are called upon to prove that we are men!

"'What, to the American slave, is your Fourth of July? I answer: a day that reveals to him, more than all other days in the year, the gross injustice and cruelty to which he is the constant victim. To him, your celebration is a sham; your boasted liberty, an unholy license; your national greatness, swelling vanity; your sounds of rejoicing are empty and heartless; your denunciations of tyrants, brass fronted impudence; your shouts of liberty and equality, hollow mockery; your prayers and hymns, your sermons and thanksgivings, with all your religious parade, and solemnity, are, to him, mere bombast, fraud, deception, impiety, and hypocrisy—a thin veil to cover up crimes which would disgrace a nation of savages. There is not a nation on the earth guilty of practices, more shocking and bloody, than are the people of these United States, at this very hour.

"'Go where you may, search where you will, roam through all the monarchies and despotisms of the old world, travel through South America, search out every abuse, and when you have found the last, lay your facts by the side of the everyday practices of this nation, and you will say with me, that, for revolting barbarity and shameless hypocrisy, America reigns without a rival.'"

"This is like evidence given by a witness against his own people,"[4] Mourid commented.

"You should say instead, evidence given by someone stung by America in its own lair," I said. "And I only read you a few of the published excerpts!"

I folded up our copy of the *New York Times* and we got up to head to a nearby coffee shop. We walked down North Pleasant Street, the main road in the town. We passed by the First National Bank of Amherst across from the Lord Jeffrey Inn and the police station, a shop called Louise's Foods, and a big church. We pushed open the glass door of the café and went in.

"What's amusing, Mourid, is that Douglass's speech is printed on one side of a page in the newspaper and a photograph of the original Declaration of Independence is printed on the other."

---

4   Qur'an surat Yusuf, 26

I handed him the *New York Times* and like a schoolgirl, recited from memory the famous expression from the Declaration of Independence, "We hold these truths to be self-evident, that all men are created equal, that they are endowed by their Creator with certain unalienable Rights, that among these are Life, Liberty and the Pursuit of Happiness."

Mourid finished reading from paper, "That to secure these rights, Governments are instituted among Men, deriving their just powers from the consent of the governed. That whenever any Form of Government becomes destructive of these ends, it is the Right of the People to alter or abolish it, and to institute new Government, laying its foundation on such principles and organizing its powers in such form, as to them shall seem most likely to affect their Safety and Happiness."

Then Mourid immersed himself in reading the rest of the document silently and didn't look up when the waitress brought us the coffee we had ordered. I reminded him of his coffee and he started drinking it while continuing to read silently. I thought about Thomas Jefferson who helped shape the Declaration of Independence in 1776 and was himself a slave owner. I recalled that the author of the 1863 Emancipation Proclamation, Abraham Lincoln, once said, in his Senate debates with Stephen Douglas, "I have no purpose to introduce political and social equality between the white and black races. There is physical difference between the two which, in my judgment, will probably forever forbid their living together upon the footing of perfect equality." I sipped my American coffee and wondered if my judgment of these American symbols lacked objectivity, being based in historical relativism. These men had shaped historical movements according to the power of their time. They were able to drive this train well, but what was the coal that powered the locomotive? "All Men are created Equal": this is the bump in the road, the contradiction. Did any of them say that "these savages"— referring to the Indigenous Peoples of this land—or "those Black devils"—are men? The text declaring independence for the thirteen

American colonies regards white settlers as the only people in the country who are "Men"! But this is a common use of words, and who dares to imprison the rain or come between the sounds of a storm and the ears of prisoners? Who dares? The eternal old man bends over his writing to record that the first of the revolutionary martyrs who fell in the Boston Massacre in 1770 was Crispus Attucks, who had mixed African and Native American origins. Word of this came as a rumor to slaves on Southern plantations; it traveled to them by the dark of night, was whispered to them in their beds, and they rushed to join the revolution that was announcing that all men were equal. The revolution's leadership allowed slaves to volunteer for its ranks in exchange for their emancipation after victory. But the world is shaped by self-interest, and the owners of plantations in the South wanted freedom for themselves, not for their slaves. They put pressure on General Washington, and he responded to this by guaranteeing to loyalists in Southern states that what rules applied to a white man didn't to a slave because he was property. After this, no slave could participate in the revolutionary army unless he was a "free negro" before his army service.

Mourid folded the newspaper, and we paid for our coffee and left. On the way, we saw American flags flying. I said, "Sometimes I wonder if I can look at America objectively. How can someone who has been stung speak with such detached calm about the characteristics of the scorpion? Where do I go when that subjugation particular to Third World people becomes much more intense, when I am so close to the experience of colonial violence and the trespasses it is built on? At times, I am struck by the manifestations of massive urbanization and some of its achievements. Then a sad little bell rings in my memory—something that Black Elk, one of the Native American Elders, once said. He had witnessed the massacre at Wounded Knee in 1890, which ended a ten-year struggle between European settlers and the Indigenous people there. He said, 'I did not know then how much was ended. When I look back now from this high hill of my old age, I can still see the butchered women and children lying heaped and scattered all along the crooked gulch as plain as when I saw them with eyes young. And I can see that something else died there in the bloody mud, and was buried in the blizzard. A people's dream died there. It was a beautiful dream... the nation's hoop is broken and scattered. There is no center any longer, and the sacred tree is dead.'"

Chapter Fourteen

"My dissertation is being bound and as soon as I have picked it up, I will send you the three required copies by post. I want to leave in two weeks, three at the most, and I hope to call the travel agent who you work with to arrange for two tickets paid by the mission, and send them to us. I'll be the one who calls them to book a trip from Bradley Airport to New York's Kennedy Airport and then on to Cairo, via Rome."

I was speaking on the telephone with the director of the Egyptian cultural bureau in Washington. His voice came through the phone line, saying, "First off, congratulations and congratulations again on the record speed it took you to get your doctorate. But why are you in such a hurry to rush back? I hope that nothing's wrong?"

"Thank you very much, I appreciate it. The situation is that I came here to accomplish very specific work, I finished it, and now I want to go back to Egypt. Then, laughingly, I said in Egyptian slang, "Doc, living outside Egypt's lonely, and I wanna go back to my country!"

He laughed too and said, "OK, Doctor… at your service!"

We began getting ready to leave. One morning, Mourid carried the big blue suitcase and I the small brown one and we took them to the central post office on Mount Pleasant Street, just a few steps from the house. Inside the post office, we opened the suitcases full of small brown parcels. For the past two days, we'd been buying dozens of strong envelopes and putting a number of books in each one. Then we wrote my name and address in Cairo on each one, also adding in big, clear letters, "Printed Matter." The postal worker gave us a large, thick cloth bag to put our parcels in after warning us that it was necessary to write the address on each individual envelope. He picked up the bag and put it on the huge scale behind the wooden counter, and then lifted it up with both hands. He closed it and stamped it and went back to his seat. He then turned to his little notebook where he kept track of communications and said, "Sixty-four pounds of printed matter."

The next evening, we were invited to dinner at my professor's house. We had fixed the time immediately after my dissertation defense. He'd invited Mourid, me, and the members of the examination committee, saying with a good-hearted smile, "A little party in honor of the little doctor. Don't forget, I will be waiting for you on the thirteenth of July."

We didn't forget the date and we probably will never forget it. The phone rang before noon, an international call.

"I am calling you from your uncle's house. Your cousin Fahim has been martyred in Chiyah, Beirut. His body arrived here and we just buried him."

Mourid's face went pale; he said nothing. He put the phone down and we sat in silence. Little details came to me. I saw Fahim's thin brown face, the traces of an old burn on his neck, his anxious adolescent eyes, and the English grammar book that I helped him study from the night before his secondary school exams a few years ago. I saw the dark cloak of death enveloping him, carrying him, and moving by. He passed away far from us. Neither of us spoke. Should we go outside? We were abroad, far from home. Should we go back home? Should we go to the professor's party? Being abroad felt intense, but nonetheless we went to his house and sat across from each other at the large table covered with a white tablecloth. Mourid sat shrunken and silent. He started shivering, so my professor gave him a jacket to wear. He ate a little, went into the bathroom, threw up, and then we left.

We prepared to travel. Media outlets carried daily stories about the war raging in Lebanon, the American news depicting it as though it were a struggle between Christians and Muslims, and reporting on the unprecedented stand of the Egyptian government, which refused to condemn Israel in an international conference. I picked up the bound copies of my dissertation and delivered them to the proper locations. Then I went to the university administration in order to request proof that I'd earned my doctorate, since I knew that the official diplomas, written in beautiful, stylized calligraphy on special paper, are only awarded twice per year. I said to the employee responsible for this, "Please send my diploma by mail to my address in Cairo. No, I won't be at the graduation ceremony, I only want an attestation saying that I earned this degree and that the official diploma will be awarded in September."

Two days later I picked up the attestation, thanked him, and left.

Chapter Fifteen

We left Amherst the morning of August 5. We were carrying two suitcases and the little typewriter I'd bought on that October day. Some of our friends accompanied us to Bradley Airport in Hartford. We bade them farewell and took the plane to New York. At seven in the evening, our Pan-Am flight took off for Rome. We spent one week in the Italian capital and then went on to Cairo, where we arrived on the evening of August 12.

That very same week, the American Secretary of State, Henry Kissinger, arrived in Cairo as well, to take care of some housekeeping inside Egypt.

When I left Cairo two years earlier, diplomatic relations between Egypt and the United States had been severed since 1967. I had gotten the entry visa for the US from the Spanish embassy that was charged with looking after American interests in Egypt. Like all students going abroad, I had to obtain signatures of approval in addition to the usual signatures of the chair of the department, the dean of the faculty, and the president of the university from the Ministry of Higher Education and the Foreign Ministry.

But in two years, life had changed. Nixon had visited Egypt and they painted the facades of the houses he was going to pass by on the way to Alexandria. (At the time, a girlfriend wrote to me with bitter sarcasm, "Perhaps the government thought it should take us in groups to shower so that we could be worthy of having Mrs. Nixon look at us. Or perhaps they thought about painting us the way they whitewashed the houses!") Eastern generosity was manifest in the extreme graciousness toward the men of the

American administration who flocked to Egypt to make deals and enjoy themselves at shows by famous dancers, with the Egyptian pyramids as the backdrop. Egyptian-American friendship was consolidated and moved toward total loyalty—the Egyptian government's loyalty, of course!

Less than three weeks after my arrival, they signed something that they called the Second Separation of Forces Agreement, whose first clause stipulates that the Egyptian and Israeli governments have agreed that the conflict between them and in the Middle East will not be resolved by military means.

On September 11 of that year, Palestine Resistance Radio in Cairo, where Mourid worked, was closed down. Egyptian media started broadcasting songs about Arab-Israeli peace. Israel was bombing South Lebanon; the Lebanese Civil War raged on with no end. Mourid left Egypt to set up Palestine Resistance Radio in Beirut. I went back to my work as a professor at the Faculty of Arts at Ain Shams University.

An administrative employee at the university asked me, "Hello, Doctor, where is your diploma?"

I answered, "If you mean the fancy piece of paper, they are sending it to me by mail because I didn't wait there to collect it. I have this attestation from the university administration. I believe it should suffice."

The employee looked at me with surprise. I handed him the attestation and left.

I followed the news of daily bombings in the Lebanese capital. I was pregnant and had a miscarriage. Mourid published a new book, which included what he talked about on his daily radio show, both in writing and his broadcasts. The name of the book was *Difficult Days*. Mourid returned to Cairo. He went back to writing and I went back to working at the university. I got pregnant again. The radio opened again but then was closed back down on the night of November 18, 1977. Sadat visited Israel that same day. On television the following evening, we watched Sadat shake

Menachem Begin and Golda Meir's hands and we listened to an Israeli military band play "Ha Tikva" and the Egyptian national anthem, which had not yet been changed from "It's Been a Long Time, My Weapon" to "My Country, Biladi." The next morning was Eid al-Adha. Five security officers knocked on our door. They had come to arrest Mourid and deport him. I bade him farewell, holding our little baby, Tamim, in my arms—he was only five months old. Despite Tamim and the two guava trees that Mourid had planted in our garden, that grew and bore fruit with surprising speed, and despite my confidence that amounted to faith that things wouldn't stay like this, I knew that the days ahead would indeed be difficult days.

Translator's Note

As a memoir, *The Journey* is a travelogue, a political statement, a feminist text, an analysis of society, and a love story. Charting Radwa Ashour's fascinating story of completing a PhD in African American poetics at the University of Massachusetts Amherst in the 1970s, the memoir is rich with literary skill, insightful analysis, and stories of its time and place. One of this text's great challenges in translation is that it is a translational text. It uses Arabic to express Ashour's experiences and reflections about studying in the United States as an Egyptian female student, activist, novelist, and scholar in the 1970s. The translation of experiences that happened in the shift from English into Arabic, and then back again, was a major challenge for me as the translator of this work.

I embarked upon the translation of *The Journey*—initially only the first chapter—when Radwa Ashour was still alive and only finished it after her premature passing. I endeavored to infuse the translation with the generosity of spirit, sharp mind, principled political commitment, and literary flair of the original Arabic version. The text of this memoir opens up a new world to its readers, by sharing Ashour's American journey in the 1970s with her Arabic language readership. I hope that I have shaped this translation in a way that similarly opens up a different world to an English language readership in 2018 and conveys the voice of how this young Egyptian feminist activist, scholar, and author conveyed her experiences at the time of her journey.

I have struggled to do justice to the privilege and responsibility of translating such a particular work, its aesthetics and literary sensibilities, its political commitment, and its 1970s worldview. I contextualize *The Journey* in more depth in the introduction that accompanies an earlier translation of this memoir's first chapter in *Comparative American Studies: An International Journal* [13:4 (2015): pp. 209-219]. I have also analyzed the particular challenges of translating this work, for example in relation to Ashour's rendition of Langston Hughes's famous poem, "Harlem (2)" in my article "Dreams Deferred, Translated: Radwa Ashour and Langston Hughes" in *CLINA: An Interdisciplinary Journal of Translation, Interpretation and Intercultural Communication*, which can be accessed at http://revistas.usal.es/index.php/clina/article/view/14554. The passage in *The Journey* where this poem occurs is one of the work's most powerful descriptions of African America and demonstrates Ashour's commitment to portraying this community in its struggles and achievements. In the original Arabic text, Radwa recites this poem, in her own Arabic translation, to her husband Mourid as they walk the streets of New York City. In this translation, however, I have referred to the recitation of the poem but for reasons of copyright it has not been reproduced in its entirety. I draw attention to this here because it is an interesting and even crucial literary moment in the Arabic memoir that is only approximated in the English version.

For many reasons, I have avoided using footnotes or a glossary in this book. The footnotes that appear here are all Ashour's, except one that points to a specific quoted verse in the Qur'an. *The Journey* is a book of its time and place and itself chooses what to and not to explain. I have chosen to allow this to come through in the translation, challenging the reader unfamiliar with references or ideas to explore them outside of the text itself. Words left in the Arabic original here are included sparingly, and then only to punctuate particular moments. For example, when Radwa and Mourid meet a Palestinian pizza maker in New York City, he greets them with words of welcome, *"Ahlein, ahlein."* This underlines Mourid's moment of connection. Radwa uniquely Arabizes the name of

New York City as *York al-jadida* in a moment when she is explaining the racial geography of the city in the 1970s.

Another feature of translating this text is the preservation of a slightly formal language and expression in the English version. Part of the beauty of Ashour's text in the original Arabic is her use of a clear and direct formal language, free of colloquialisms. This conveys the seriousness of purpose the memoir's young protagonist has in her journey. One might expect a parallel work in English—even more so were it written in the twenty-first century—to take a more informal tone, and I have opted to preserve this somewhat more formal tone to parallel the original text's style.

One further issue I would like to point to in this note is how the original text in Arabic, and this English translation, approach issues like race and racism, American Imperialism, and Third World solidarity. I have tried to capture the different language and expressions of the time. I have also tried to remain true to Third World solidarity politics of the 1970s, where African Americans and Egyptians were part of a larger worldwide struggle against racism and Imperialism. Where Ashour shows Black Americans and Egyptians to be "the same" it should be understood in this political moment and climate. Passages where her text reads differently from what we are used to reading today, particularly in relation to race and identity, reflect how different politics and political moments affect our expression, and vice versa.

It is in the spirit of bringing *The Journey* to a larger, English-speaking audience that I dedicate this translation to the memory of Radwa Ashour, the political vision she expresses so brilliantly within it, and a free Palestine.

Michelle Hartman

Translator's Acknowledgements

I worked on this translation in pieces over a long period of time. I would first and foremost like to acknowledge the brilliant Radwa Ashour for her enthusiasm about this translation and her openness to my questions about it, before she left us, too soon. I would like to also thank her family, Mourid and Tamim Barghouti, for generously allowing me to complete the project. I am grateful to Michel Moushabeck of Interlink Books for believing in this project and making sure it saw the light of day. Thanks to everyone at Interlink for their hard work on it.

Rasheed El-Enany introduced this memoir to me, many years ago, and he and Rabab Abdulhadi encouraged me to work on it. Thanks to you both. Thanks also to Rula Jurdi, Dima Ayoub, Yasmine Nachabe and most especially Ghiwa Abihaidar for their help in the translation process. They all discussed it with me at some length and Ghiwa deserves many thanks for her consistent work. My deep thanks extend to the McGill students who helped me think through the translation and also commented upon in it an earlier stage: Ralph Haddad, Niyousha Bastani, Chantelle Schultz, Maxine Dannat, Isabelle Oke, and Sara Sebti. Ira Dworkin and Ebony Coletu helped me work on the translation of the first chapter that was published in *Comparative American Studies: An International Journal* (13:4, 2015). I thank them as well as Marcia Lynx Qualey for their commitment to the project and help in getting the full translation published and publicized. My thanks as always to another Tameem, who is helping me more and more complete my translation projects.